100 GARDEN GAMES

100 GARDEN GAMES

BY SIDNEY G. HEDGES

FIRST PUBLISHED IN 1936

hamlyn

An Hachette Livre UK Company
www.hachettelivre.co.uk

First published in Great Britain in 1936

This revised edition published in 2008 by
Hamlyn, a division of Octopus Publishing Group Ltd
2–4 Heron Quays, London E14 4JP
www.octopusbooks.co.uk

ISBN 978-0-600-61840-9

A CIP catalogue record for this book is available from the British Library

Printed and bound in Shanghai

2 4 6 8 10 9 7 5 3 1

AUTHOR'S NOTE

Don't pay too much attention to the Chapter divisions of this book. It was necessary to get some sort of classification for easy reference. But very often a game of one section could equally well have been included in another. *Toss Ball*, for example (No. 73), would have been quite suitable in either of the other games chapters. It was placed among 'games for larger parties,' simply because there are fewer games which can be fairly included in this category.

For quick searching the chapter headings will help you, but when you have time choose games for your special needs from the whole book.

I am most grateful to Messrs. F. H. Ayres, the well-known manufacturers of sports and games requisites, for the help they have given me in the preparation of this book, and similarly to John Jaques and Son, and A. G. Spalding and Bros.

SIDNEY G. HEDGES
BICESTER, OXON

A NOTE ON THIS EDITION

The text for this edition remains completely unchanged from that which was published in 1936. Some of the games will seem quaint, others bewildering, but many of them will remind older readers of their own childhoods – lazy summers spent playing in the garden and exploring the world around them with their chums. This book will take you back to those more innocent times, before television and computer games, when entertainment was a wholesome family activity that required imagination and effort.

There are suggestions for 100 garden games within this book that, even seven decades on, are great fun to play. Some may not be too practical – perhaps taking up rather more space than you have – but they still provide a charming insight into a time when gardens were large and most people had a serviceable knowledge of croquet and badminton.

It's important to emphasize that attitudes towards health and safety have changed since this book was first published over 70 years ago. This is a defiantly no-nonsense approach to fun and, whilst it makes for absorbing reading, we cannot recommend any responsible parent condones such activities as archery, lariat and boomerang throwing if it isn't properly supervised.

To give you a helping hand we have provided new illustrations for some of the more complex ideas and others with which you may not be familiar. Otherwise the book is as it was printed in 1936 and serves as great reference for outdoor fun and also as a piece of social history, a window into an austere-but-content Britain – utterly fascinating and extremely charming.

CONTENTS

CHAPTER FOUR:

Games For The Children

DIAGRAMS

CHAPTER ONE

GAMES FOR ONE OR TWO PLAYERS

1 ARCHERY

This fine old pastime can be very delightful in a garden. You may shoot over 15, 20, or 25 yards, and the size of your target may vary with the range – from 2 to 4 ft. in diameter. Your bow should be as long as you are tall; though if a number of people are to use the same bow, one of medium size will best serve for all.

Only string your bow for actual shooting, or the constant strain on the stick will spoil it. To string the bow, put the end of the stick against the inner side of your foot, the loop of one end of the bow-string being in the notch at this end of the stick. Slide the other loop up the stick with your right hand as far as it will go. Then, holding the middle of the stick firmly with the left hand, force the top away from you with the right, at the same time sliding the string's loop up with the same hand until it slips into the top notch.

To shoot, grip the handle of the bow with the left hand and hold the stick vertical in front of you, the left side of your body being turned towards the target. The string must be drawn back with the fleshy parts of the three finger ends – the little finger and the thumb do not assist but are curled into the palm. The arrow is notched on to the string, and its end rests between the first and second fingers, though they do not grip it. The shaft of the arrow passes to the left of the bow stick, lying on the ledge formed by the joint of the first finger of the left hand. To loose off the arrow the right-hand fingers simply straighten, thus releasing the cord which springs forward driving the arrow with it.

Draw back clean to the chin, and release immediately, without any pause or stiffening tension.

As your head is above the arrow level, you can aim straight by looking along the shaft and getting it in line with the target, but you cannot sight it similarly for the horizontal level. To achieve this you must aim at a point well above the target if the range is long. Only experience and practice will teach you how high to aim.

At the moment of the draw the right forearm should be in line with the arrow.

Scoring on an archery target is reckoned as follows: the 'bull' (generally termed the 'gold') 9 points, and the succeeding outer rings 7, 5, 3, 1 – their colours generally being red, blue, black, white.

2 BOX BALL

Though this game naturally makes a special appeal to the person fond of boxing, it is a game which can give enjoyment and, if desired, quite strenuous exercise to any person. And you play it by yourself.

The necessary equipment – consisting of band to go round the head, length of rubber, with light punching-ball on the end – can be bought easily enough, under a variety of names. If you care to make your own outfit, get a piece of webbing or broad tape which can be looped or buckled round the head. At the point in the middle of the forehead a 2-ft. length of strong elastic or thin catapult rubber is fastened; and to the other end of this a light ball or rubber bladder 6 to 9 in. in diameter is secured. That is the full equipment.

All you have to do now is to box the ball. Each time you punch it the rubber will bring it back again towards your face. Both hands, of course, will be used, and you may dodge and parry with as much vigour as you like.

Though you may use the ball on quite a small patch of lawn, there is much more fun if you have freedom for footwork.

As your skill develops so will the variety and interest of the game. You may, for instance, dodge just as the ball is likely to hit your head, so that the ball passes over your shoulder; then, as the rubber brings it springing back at you, you can twist round and face it once more.

If you would have a competitive interest, see how many times the ball gets out of your control, or touches your body, within a fixed time – perhaps two minutes.

Two practised players, each with a box ball, can set to work close to each other, and have the added complication of dodging each other's balls.

3 BUCKET QUOITS

Put a bucket on the ground, and mark one, or two, throwing lines. The distance of the lines from the bucket should be 10 ft. for ladies, 15 ft. for men. From this line rope quoits are thrown, in an endeavour to get them into the bucket.

When two or more players are taking part each in turn sends up four rings. One point is reckoned for each quoit or ring that goes into the bucket. A ring lodging on the edge does not count – unless later it is dislodged and so falls into the bucket, thus gaining an ordinary point.

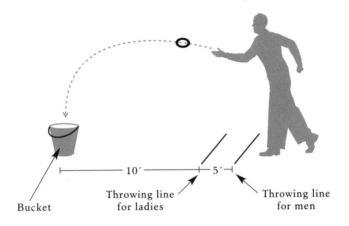

Bucket   Throwing line   Throwing line
                  for ladies   for men

Twenty-one points make *game*. If two players tie at '20-all,' one of them must secure two successive points before he can win.

Failing quoit rings, balls or beanbags may be used. The method of making beanbags is described in *Chapter 5*.

4 DIABOLO

This ancient game is never out of date; revivals have occurred many times in many countries during the last century or so – since the game was rediscovered from Roman sources. The simple equipment of sticks and double cone or top is always readily procurable.

At first diabolo is for the single player. Two can take part only when both have attained considerable skill.

The common error of beginners is to hold the sticks too widely apart, and to work both arms up and down in seesaw fashion. The right way is to keep both sticks close together, and to move only one hand.

To start, put your double cone on the ground, with the string passing under its waist. Hold the sticks side by side in front of you, so that the two parts of the string rise vertically and parallel with each other. Now, keeping the left arm and stick motionless, begin to raise and lower the right stick with a quick, whipping action, taking care not to spread the stick outwards away from the left arm. Gradually the top will begin to revolve, with growing force. As its velocity increases so it becomes more and more steady on the string, and soon it will be spinning so fast that a distinct humming note will be audible.

It is well that you should understand just how the spinning is set up. The right stick whips upward, making the top revolve to the left. Then the right stick falls, and the top drops too, without, however, having its spinning much impeded. Then comes another upward flick of the right stick, which augments the right to left spinning of the top. Each flick of the stick further increases the top's momentum. Obviously, if the left stick is jerked up alternately with the right the effect is to impart first a left to right and then a right to left spin – with the result that the top fails to rotate at all and drops inert to the ground.

The holding together of the sticks results in more of the string touching the waist of the top, not only helping the more to steady it, but giving a better grip to assist the spinning.

When your double cone is revolving really strongly you may flick your sticks upwards and outwards suddenly, so that the string becomes taut and the top is tossed into the air. The spinning will keep it steady and horizontal during its flight, and when it falls you must catch it on the taut string, which will immediately be allowed to come down into its original position so that the top can be 'whipped' up to a good speed once again.

When two players take part the top can be tossed backwards and forwards between them. Understanding the one-way spin of the top, you will appreciate that if your partner is facing you when he catches your top he will need to work his left instead of his right hand when speeding up the spin, if he is to keep the top revolving in the same direction. Once have this clear in your mind and you will avoid the puzzlement of players who cannot understand why the top falls dead when the receiver checks or reverses the spin by working the wrong stick.

5 FIVE-TEN

Developed from *fives* and *tennis*, this game combines many good qualities of both. Ordinary tennis rackets and balls are used, and the necessary back-board can be bought from a sports dealer, or easily made.

The court is marked out as in the diagram on page 21 – in which the dimensions given are of maximum size. If your lawn has not sufficient space for these measurements, your court may be reduced to even a quarter of this size without the game being seriously hampered; though, naturally, if the court is half as long and half as wide the vigour and scope of play will be much lessened.

Divide your court lengthways and across, into four equal sections. The two front sections are *service courts*, into which the ball must rebound after a service – unless it has been 'pocketed.'

The board should be rather less wide than the court, though it may be of equal width if the court be narrow. It consists of a frame which stands or fixes firmly upright. The bottom part is a strip of net 3 ft. high – like a tennis net; the top half is a 3 ft. strip of black wood. In the middle of this wood, at the bottom edge, is a sort of 'letter-box' slit, 6 in. deep and 2 ft. wide. Behind this slit or pocket is a net or box to catch balls that pass through.

Two or four players can take part. Play follows the general lines of tennis as much as possible, reckoning their scores 15, 30, and so on. Services are taken from alternate back corners. If you prefer, you may use the general Net Game Rules given at the end of this book.

Each server plays his ball at the back-board, hoping to get through the slit into the pocket. If this is achieved one point is counted. If not pocketed the ball should bounce back into the service court of the opponent, otherwise it is a faulty service. Two services are allowed. If both are bad a point is lost.

After the service play goes on as in tennis. The object of the game is to pocket the ball. Each player, or side, if four are taking

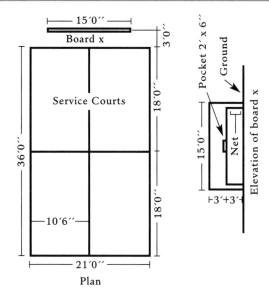

Plan

part, plays the ball in turn. When the ball drops outside the court, or goes into the net under the backboard, or falls to the ground and is not returned, then a point is lost. It is not necessary, of course, that the ball shall rebound into a particular service court except for services.

If you find that the ball often misses the board altogether, and has to be recovered from all over the garden, then put up a tall net right across behind the board, and even round the sides too – like the netting round a tennis court.

Hard hitting and volleying naturally have their part in the game, for if a stroke of yours fails to get the pocket you will hope that the ball will return in such a manner as to be unplayable by your opponent.

One rule needs rigid enforcement until you become proficient – no player must obstruct an opponent. If you get in the way of a ball coming to your opponent you forfeit a point to him.

A single player can get plenty of enjoyment from *five-ten*.

6 FLY BALL

Two take part in this. Stretched between them is a length of elastic cord or rubber – about 10 ft.; and from the middle is suspended a large, light ball, or a sturdy rubber bladder. The ends of the main cord may be fastened to the waists of the players, or each end may have a handgrip which can be held by the player.

The object of each person is to make the ball hit his opponent, and to effect this he springs and feints around the other, jerking the ball towards him, and punching or striking it whenever opportunity offers.

Both players are thus continuously dodging, and pretty strenuous exertion results.

Every time the ball touches a player a point is counted; and *game* is 5 points.

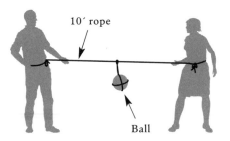

10′ rope

Ball

7 JUGGLING BALLS

Ball juggling is a fascinating pastime, and there is no better place for practising than in the garden – where no breakages can occur. It is only possible to introduce the beginnings of the pastime here.

Solid or sponge rubber balls, of golf size, are most suitable, though tennis balls will serve.

Begin by taking a ball in one hand and tossing and catching it many times. Make it rise vertically to a height of about 3 ft. Do not move your hand for the catch, if the ball has gone straight up it will come down straight. Continue until you can catch it just as surely with your eyes shut. Each hand must be trained similarly.

Next try tossing from one hand to the other. Hold both out in front, and toss the ball across, so that it rises from 2 to 3 ft. and falls cleanly into the other hand. Then toss back. Your concern must be to toss with such precision that the balls falls into the hand without the hand moving.

Following this you may toss the ball across in the same fashion, from in front of the right hip, for example, and then carry the right hand across swiftly to the left hip so that it catches the ball instead of letting the left hand take it. Immediately toss back again from the right hand and carry the same hand back to its original position to make the catch. Do this same work with the left hand. Repeat all such exercises over and over again – remember it is not quickness of eye and movement that must allow you to make catches, but mechanically accurate throwing which enables you to know exactly where the ball will fall.

It is now time for you to tackle two balls simultaneously. Take one in each hand and throw them up together, taking care that they rise to the same height, for it is important that each hand shall be able to throw with the same strength. Catch the balls with the same hands. After a while send the balls up alternately, so that the left is always rising while the right is falling, and vice versa.

You can now try two balls with a single hand. Take the two in the right hand, and toss one straight up. The instant that it begins to descend the other ball will be thrown. Clearly neither must be thrown quite vertically, or they would collide. Each is tossed so that it describes a narrow arch, and falls clear of its fellow. The hand thus moves just a few inches to make each catch, then recovers to make the next throw. One ball is caught just at the instant the other is at its highest point. To allow yourself plenty of time, make fairly high throws, but as you gain skill the tosses may be reduced to about 2 ft.

It is really not so very difficult when you have mastered

two-ball juggling with each hand to work both hands together, using four balls at the same time.

Just one more stage – three-ball juggling.

The three balls all travel round in the same direction.

To start, hold the left hand about a foot higher than the right, and have one ball in the left hand and two in the right. Toss the right-hand ball fairly high. When it is up follow with the second right-hand ball. The right hand is now empty, so the left tosses the third ball down into it. This third is not retained, but promptly tossed up by the right hand – by which time the left hand has caught the first ball and tossed it down towards the right hand, thus the left is again empty and able to receive the second ball. So it goes on, the balls following each other round, remaining evenly spaced.

8 LA GRACE

This is a graceful old French game which, like *diabolo*, is constantly coming into popularity again. The equipment can be bought, or improvised with very little trouble.

Two players take part. Each is provided with two smooth sticks, rather like slim, shortened billiard cues. Two rings of cane or smooth wood are also needed, one of 6 in. diameter and the other of 4 in. These are just approximate sizes. Each ring should be of medium weight – a thick curtain ring, for instance, is too clumsy, but a flimsy hoop is equally useless.

The players stand at an agreed distance from each other, perhaps 20 ft. Each has a stick in each hand, and the points of the sticks are crossed through the ring. The sticks are held to the front, pointing slightly upwards and towards the opposing player. Then, at a mutually arranged signal, each pulls his sticks sharply apart, flicking outward with each hand. This causes the ring to shoot forward.

The aim of each player is to catch the other's ring on his own sticks. To make a catch both sticks are held forward as before, but now with points together. As the hands are apart the ring cannot slide far up the two sticks, and it is thus ready for an immediate return.

Until some proficiency is attained, this catching of each other's rings will take all your attention and skill. But later it may be your aim also to make the smaller ring pass through the large one in flight.

Players should not move about the lawn, but keep their places as much as possible. To get competitive interest, one point may be reckoned for each successful catch, and *game* can be 25 points.

For a variation let one player send the big ring high into the air, and let the second try to propel the small ring through it as it descends.

9 LAWN HOCKEY

The 'field' is a long narrow strip, 3½ ft. wide and anything up to 40 ft. long. Straight lines on the turf must show the side boundaries. At each end are the 'goals,' formed by two sticks or pegs in the ground 15 in. apart.

Two or four players can take part – only two if the playing space is short. With four, one player on each side stays back near the goal, while his fellow plays forward.

Ordinary hockey sticks and ball are used. To start the game the ball is bullied off at the centre – the opposing players standing

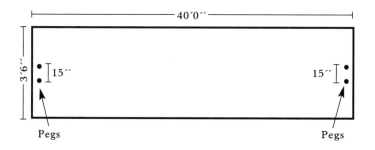

on opposite sides of the ball, touching their sticks twice above it after having touched the ground on their own sides, then striking at the ball.

Play proceeds as nearly as possible as in field hockey. Goals are scored and restarts made as in the ordinary game. Whenever the ball goes outside the boundaries it is brought in and played from a point opposite the spot where it went out.

No player is allowed to step inside the field of play. As opponents are on opposite sides of the 'field' they do not impede each other. Strength does not count much, but quickness and neat control of the ball are the essential qualities for good play.

10 MID-COURT BALL

This is an easily planned game of tennis type, though no net is required. Instead of a net a middle court separates the opposing players, who play a tennis ball backwards and forwards, with wooden padders – see *Chapter 5* – or tennis rackets.

If padders are used, the measurements of the court should be approximately those given in the accompanying diagram; with rackets the court may be proportionately bigger, as the ball will be driven with greater ease.

It will be seen that with a court 6 ft. wide the end courts will each be square and the middle court 12 ft. long. This is a size suitable for singles play; for doubles the width should be about half as much again.

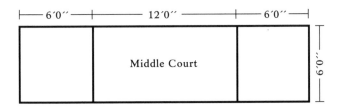

As far as possible the rules for *Net Games*, at the end of this book, should be used, though it is immaterial where a player stands to make his service, so long as he is on or behind his rear line.

The service and every other stroke must make the ball to bounce in the mid-court. The ball should bounce here only once, and should then travel on and bounce again in the end court – unless it is played back by a volley before it can touch the ground. The point is lost if the ball bounces more than once in either mid- or end court, or of course if it fails to come inside its proper court.

The game is not so easy as at first may appear, for the player has two things to consider in making a stroke – the ball must not only bounce in the mid-court, but must bounce a second time in the opponent's end – if the opponent cares to let it. This necessity greatly complicates the type of strokes necessary, and finesse rather than hard hitting becomes necessary.

11 PADDER BADMINTON

This is plain badminton, except that padders, described in *Chapter 5*, are used instead of rackets, and consequently the shuttles do not travel so far. The game is useful where space is so restricted that a full-size court is not possible, and yet freer play than *tether-shuttle* allows is desired.

Using padders allows a court even half as long and half as broad as standard size to be used.

Sturdy outdoor shuttles are most serviceable, and the strong rubber base gives considerable elasticity and yet withstands hard hitting.

Ordinary badminton rules, outlined for game No. 36 can be used, or the simple *Net Game Rules* in the last chapter of the book.

12 PEG QUOITS

Quoit boards, with one or more pegs sticking upright, are easily obtained, and serve for the commonest form of this popular garden game. Rope quoit rings are used, and are thrown from a suitable distance. If two or more persons are taking part they may play either individually or as sides. In the former circumstance one player at a time takes the four quoits and endeavours to throw them each over the peg or pegs – the total number of points being marked to his score. If there is one peg, each 'ringer' scores a point; if several pegs the appropriate number will be marked on the board. Any quoit must rest completely over a peg if the score is to count. When sides or teams participate the players each use the four quoits, or any agreed lesser number, in turn, and total the score when all have finished. The player or side whose total score first reaches a previously agreed number – perhaps 100 – wins the game. First play is decided by tossing.

But if you desire to play the game in more serious fashion you may fix an iron peg, about 10 inches high, in the end of your lawn, or one at each end – a convenient way of doing this is described in *Chapter 5*. An official quoit rink consists of a piece of ground 75 ft. long and 10 ft. wide. Naturally this length can be adjusted to the convenience of your garden.

Four quoit rings should be used if you have one peg; eight if you have two. The advantage of having two is that players can receive the rings thrown by their opponents, and thus save the trouble of fetching them back for the next set of throws.

A throwing line must be marked if you have but one peg. With two pegs the player stands in line with the near peg, at one side, and not more than 2 ft. from it. The ground in front of this mark must not be touched when a throw is made, and neither foot must be in front of it.

Each player throws his four rope or rubber quoits, and then points are awarded as follows; all the rings lying where they fall:
1 point to the player having the nearest quoit to the peg.

2 points to the player having the nearest two quoits.

3 points to the player having a quoit leaning against the peg.

5 points for any quoit which encircles the peg.

Clearly, when players are taking part from each end of the 'rink,' there must always be two opponents playing from the same end.

Game consists of 21 points, and *set* or *match* of the best two out of three games. With double-end play players change ends at the close of each game, and in a third game when 10 points have been scored by either side.

13 PLATE SPINNING

You may have admired a stage juggler, but perhaps you have never thought of trying any of his tricks. Well, the garden is an ideal place for a little plate spinning.

You need an ordinary enamelled plate, and a light stick about two feet long, with its end sharpened to a rounded point.

Now put this pointed stick-end against the concave edge of the plate, and, holding the stick vertical, work it round and round, rapidly, with a circular movement of the wrist.

This will set the plate spinning flatly, and after a little practice you will be able to keep it balanced horizontally on the top of your upright stick. Your wrist movement must be very swift and smooth. The lower end of the stick, where you are holding it, should scarcely move at all, and the circle described by the pointed tip need be no more than a few inches in diameter.

At first the edge of the plate will prevent the stick from slipping. As you become more skilful, you will be able to bring the stick's point nearer the middle of the plate, thus reducing the sweep of the stick and giving better speed and steadiness.

The next stage of proficiency will be reached when you can toss the plate up and catch it again on the stick. Following this you may start off by tossing the plate into the air, imparting a rotary movement to it as you do so, then catching it on the point of your stick and immediately augmenting the spin by the familiar twirl of the stick.

With a stick in each hand it will be possible to toss the spinning plate from right hand to left, and back; and later still you may spin two plates simultaneously.

Further, you may go on to balance the stick on your chin when the plate is spinning strongly, and so on – but things of that sort can be left to your personal exploration.

14 POLE PUNCH

This is a strenuous game for two players. The equipment can either be made, or it can be adapted from a *pole tennis* outfit, which can be bought from a sports dealer – under any of half a dozen names, like *tether ball*, *spiral pole*, *bumble puppy*. The method of erecting a pole in a rigid socket is described in the last chapter of this book. It is a very good plan to use the pole for pole punch and the next two games as well (15 and 16). The best height for your pole will then be 10 ft., but for pole punch itself it need be no more than 8 ft. out of the ground.

From the top of the pole suspend by a light but strong cord a large ball that will stand up to hard punching. A light football may serve, or a strong rubber bladder, of the sort that has reinforcing strips of material at intervals round it. When at rest the ball should hang within a couple of feet of the ground. Six feet from the ground, or less if the pole be short, a mark should be painted round the pole.

To begin the game the two players stand on opposite sides of the pole, at least a yard out. One of them holds the ball, and he starts by punching it hard, in an endeavour to make it circle round the pole.

One player punches in a clockwise direction, the other counter-clockwise. It is the aim of each to drive the ball round and round until the cord is wound completely on the pole, *above the mark*.

There is no waiting for turns; each punches whenever he can reach the ball – though taking care to remain on his own side of the pole. Thus the cord is constantly winding and unwinding, and in a hard contest each lap round the pole is gained after struggle. Should the cord or ball touch the pole, or coil round it, below the mark it is lifted clear and a free punch taken by the player whose opponent was responsible for the fault. It is a similar fault for the cord to become entangled in the hand or arm of a player.

15 POLE SKITTLES

The same pole is needed as for the previous game, the preparation of which is described in *Chapter 5*, but this time a tennis ball must be tethered to the end of the string – the manner of effecting this is also dealt with in the same chapter.

Around the pole stand a number of skittles or bottles, and if possible draw a circle on the ground, with a radius of about 4 ft.

Two or more players take part. Each in turn holds the ball, standing outside the marked ring, and looses it so that it swings downward and forward among the skittles. The next player does not take his turn until the ball has come to rest. That player wins who first knocks over twenty skittles.

Skittles should not be replaced until all have been knocked down. Thus play continues until none is standing, and then the succeeding player has the whole lot up again.

16 POLE TENNIS

The same equipment as for the two preceding games is needed – the pole and socket and tethered ball are fully described in *Chapter 5*. A tennis ball, of course, will be needed, as this is a real tennis game, with ordinary rackets.

The two players stand facing each other on opposite sides of the pole, and one to two yards out from it. These relative positions must be retained throughout, so that rackets do not come into collision. It is the aim of one player to drive the ball round in a clockwise direction, and the other in a counter-clockwise. Whenever the ball touches the pole below the 6-ft. mark, or the cord coils round, a fault is given, and a free hit awarded. The game is not over until the cord is completely wound up and the ball has come to rest against the pole and above the mark.

Hard and fast hitting is required for this game, for when the ball is circling in favour of a player he needs to make his racket overtake it, travelling in the same direction, in order to strike and augment its rotation. Much skill can be brought into play by tipping the ball slightly upwards, so that it just passes out of reach of an opponent, though still coiling round the pole in the desired fashion.

There is hardly a finer game for restricted garden space than pole tennis. It is not even necessary to play it on turf, for the ball never touches the ground.

It is possible for two teams of two to take part in pole tennis. It will be necessary to draw a straight line along the ground, running through the base of the pole, this will separate the territory of the opponents – the line may be useful even when just two are playing. A service point can also be fixed in each half, from which free hits will be made. In this team-play each member in turn steps forward and takes a stroke, or plays right through with a single opponent.

17 RING TOSS

With a rubber quoit or *tenikoit* ring you may have a great deal of enjoyment and exercise even when you are alone.

The more space you have the better, but your first play involves almost no moving about.

Stand still, with the ring in one hand. Toss the ring up from the right; catch it in the left hand; toss with the left; catch in the right, and so continue. Gradually increase the height of your throws, and persevere until you can maintain an even, rhythmic action, without so much as the movement of a foot being necessary.

Then try walking forward, tossing and catching first in one hand, then the other, then in alternate hands. As you gain skill you may walk faster, and later on do the same thing while running. Good judgment is necessary before you will be able to keep up a good speed without any faltering or change.

You may even go on to walking or running backwards, still tossing the ring – but be sure you know what is behind you, for there is no chance of seeing where you are going when your eye is on the ring.

18 SLIDE-BALL PUNCH

This bears the same relation to the next game (19) as *pole punch* does to *pole tennis*. It is a game that needs length, but little width, in the field of play, and it can even be played along a garden path.

Fix two sturdy posts, with 15 to 40 ft. between them. Each must stand about 8 ft. out of the ground, and must be capable of withstanding the strain of having a wire stretched tautly between them, fastened at their tops.

On this wire a smooth ring must be threaded, which will slide along easily – it may even be possible to use a small wheel

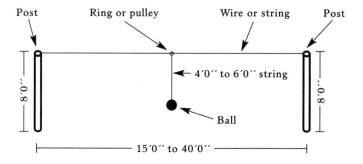

pulley, providing that once it is on it cannot fall or slip off. To the ring attach a 4- to 6-ft. length of cord, and to the end of this fasten a small football, or any ball or rubber bladder that will withstand hard punching.

The game begins with the ball at the middle. The two players stand facing each other, on opposite sides of it. They toss for the start, and the winning one takes the ball and gives it a hard punch. Then the play goes on without interruption.

It is the aim of each player to drive the ball along – the ring sliding on the wire allows this – until it touches his opponent's post. That scores a point; and the game is restarted from the middle. Five points give *game*. After each point the one who has scored should take the free punch at the centre; but each should take it in turn to start a game.

When a player gets any part of his body entangled in the cord a fault is given and the opponent takes a free punch.

19 SLIDE TENNIS

The same 8-ft. posts, and taut wire between, with ring threaded on and 4 to 6 ft. cord attached, are needed as in the preceding game. But this time to the end of the cord a tennis ball must be fastened – the manner of securing it is described in the last chapter of this book.

Two players take part. Each has a tennis racket – and one thing they must guard against is letting their rackets collide, for there is no net between to keep them apart.

A start is made at the centre. One player holds the ball, and takes a free hit – then uninterrupted play follows, unless, indeed, one gets racket or arm entangled in the cord and so gives a free hit to the opponent.

Each time the ball touches the post at either end a point is scored, and the first to get five points wins the game. After each point the player who has scored takes a free hit from the centre; and each player in turn starts off a new game.

Should your wire be short, then players may be compelled to remain on their own side of the centre mark; but with a long wire it is permissible for them to follow up the ball.

Of course, a point is scored equally if the ring or the ball touches the post.

20 SLIPPITY

Shuffleboard is a very popular game on board ship, and *slippity* is an ingenious adaptation of it for the garden.

A smooth, level strip of ground is needed, and along this is stretched a length of smooth material which can be pegged down round its edges and so held taut, to give an even, slippery surface. Strong canvas may be used, a length of old linoleum, or, less satisfactorily, a piece of old stair carpet turned upside down. A better plan is to buy a roll of properly prepared material from a sports dealer. Similarly, the slippity cues and discs may also be bought – or you may fashion your own. Eight discs of heavy wood are needed, each measuring about 3 in. across and 1 in. thick. The discs should be of four colours, two discs of each colour. In addition, one or more cues are needed. A cue is a stick or pole

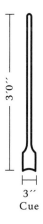

3′0″

3″
Cue

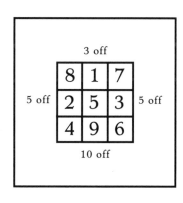

3 off

8	1	7
2	5	3
4	9	6

5 off   5 off

10 off

Numbered squares
are each 12″ x 12″

3 ft. long, with a flattened piece of wood at its end, shaped so that it grips the discs.

The cue, with the target, which must be painted or chalked on the end of the material, is shown in the diagram.

Two, three or four players can take part in slippity. Skill, chance, exercise, all combine to make the game exceedingly attractive.

The pegged-out material is called the 'rink,' and it is particularly important that there be no creases or wrinkles at the 'striking' end, or these will cause the material to wear out quickly.

The object of the game is to drive the discs to the target, and to obtain the highest number of points on the scoring area. The rink should be about 8 yds. long.

To propel the disc, it is placed on the starting line, at the near end of the rink, and the player stands just behind it with left foot well forward, and the concave end of the cue fitted against the back of the disc. Then, with a strong forward lunge and thrust, the disc is driven up the rink. The drive should be smooth and long – not a mere poke or knock.

Game can consist of 50 or 100 points, and there is more fun if the number must be scored exactly. Any score over the exact number required can then be deducted instead of being added. For instance, if in a game of 50 a player has scored 49 and his next thrust registers 9, then this 9 should be deducted instead of added, leaving him with only 40.

The first thrust at the game opening is decided by toss, or mutually; after that the winner of one game always starts the game that follows. Each player sends up one disc, followed by the other player or players in rotation, until all the discs have been sent. Should only two players be taking part each will naturally have two pairs of discs.

Scores are only counted when all the discs have been sent up to the target, so that it is the final lie of a disc that matters – its first position may be altered by a subsequent shot.

After each round the new round is started by the player

who previously went second. Discs must be wholly inside the numbered areas to score; a disc counts nothing if it is touching a line. No disc can be replayed, within a round, which has gone off the rink or missed the target. No disc must be started from any point in front of the starting line.

A disc coming to rest in the penalty space around the target loses 5 points in either of the side areas; 10 points in the front area; 3 points in the back area; and 3 points if it stops anywhere else, or goes off the rink. Discs lying in the penalty areas are at once removed.

Preferably, squares and penalty areas should measure about a foot across. With a narrower rink the penalty areas of the side may be omitted.

21 SOLO TENNIS

Equipment for this game is readily procurable, under such names as 'tennis trainer' or 'tennis tutor,' for the most common use of the game is as training for lawn tennis. But, because it is intended for a single player, the game is of considerable interest and value *per se*.

To make the equipment yourself is fairly simple. First you need two upright posts – ordinary tennis-surround uprights, 9 ft. high, will serve, though you will do better to have 10-ft. posts. Unless the posts are strong and permanent, have them kept rigid by cords and pegs. The posts should be about 10 ft. apart. Between the two tops of the posts fasten a good-quality rubber thread, only

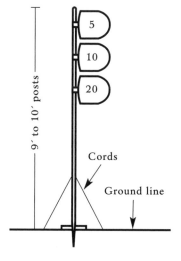

slightly stretched; and from the middle of this hang another rubber thread to the end of which a tennis ball is secured – methods of tethering a ball are described in *Chapter 5*. The ball, when at rest, should be suspended about 2 ft. from the ground.

Your equipment is now complete. All you need is a tennis racket and you can begin play. Strike the ball in just the same fashion, forehand or backhand, as in ordinary lawn tennis. The rubber will check the flight of the ball and bring it back to you with as much force as you like. Very accurate strokes are needed if you would be quite sure of the return of the ball, and you will find the mastery of the game and the experimenting with various types of strokes to be most fascinating.

It is possible to buy a sort of target, consisting of three plates fixed one above the other, at which you may aim your shots. The lowest plate, which would be hit by a ball that normally would just skim a tennis net, gives the highest score; the higher plates, equivalent to less valuable strokes, gives correspondingly lower scores. The diagram shows the appliance.

22 SQUARE BALL

This is about as simple and easily improvised a game as one can have. Any large ball that bounces well will serve. The only other requirement is a square marked out with corner stones or pegs, or lines. If the square can be pretty big, about 4 yds. across, the best game can be had; but lesser measurements will not prevent plenty of good play.

Two players take part. One stands on each side of the square, and they throw the ball backwards and forwards, making it bounce each time inside the square. The ball should not be punched or hit, but caught and thrown again without any pause. Of course, the aim of each player is so to throw the ball that his opponent is unable to catch or return it.

A point is reckoned every time a fault occurs – when the ball bounces more than once in the square, or touches the ground

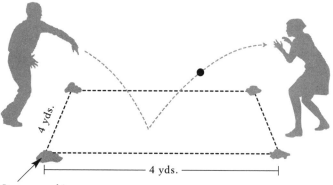

4 yds.

4 yds.

Stones marking corners

outside the square, or bounces out of the side of the square instead of over the back line. It is a fault also for a ball to be thrown in over a side line, or to fail to bounce at all.

After each fault the player who has lost the point receives the ball from his opponent's free throw.

The first to get 11 points wins the game. You may, alternatively, use the full Net Game Rules given in the last chapter of this book, in so far as they can apply.

23 SWINGBALL

This is rather like *fly ball*, No. 6, but the equipment is more easily made, as no rubber or elastic is needed. It is a magnificently strenuous and exciting game for two players, and is suitable for a lawn of even small size.

First get a 10-ft. length of strong but supple cord, and to each end secure a 5-in. length of broom-handle or similar wood, to form a handgrip. On this cord thread a ring which will slide easily and yet withstand plenty of strain. To the ring attach a 10-in. piece of cord, and at the end of this fasten a light, small football, or similar ball of fair size. The equipment is now complete.

10′ cord

Ball

Two players take part. Each holds one of the handgrips in one hand, and then they proceed to fling and snatch each in an endeavour to make the ball travel along the cord and touch the opponent.

A fair amount of practice is needed before good control is obtained, but once the knack is gained it is possible to send the ball hurtling along by a quick snatch or snaking fling, or to check a threatening rush of the ball by grounding the cord at the crucial moment.

Thus the two players are kept springing and dodging in constant, strenuous movement – until the contest is over and a 'hit' is scored. For each hit a point is counted, and that player wins the game who first scores five points.

24 SWORD TENNIS

The net for this game must be 6 ft. high; and the court divided into four equal sections – as shown in the diagram.

The sections of court immediately on either side of the net are not used at all; all the play is in the back halves.

Two players take part. Each is provided with a 'sword' – which is a smooth walking-stick of moderate weight. They toss a small wooden hoop, of about 12 in. diameter, backwards and forwards across the net. It is an advantage for each player to wear a glove on his 'sword hand,' to safeguard against possible scratches from the hoop.

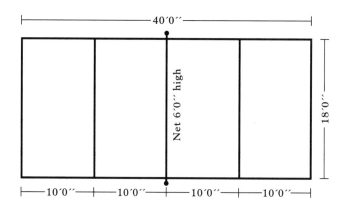

To begin the game one player threads the hoop on his stick, which he holds stretched behind him at about the level of his waist. Then, with a round-arm sweep, he brings the stick over to the front, flinging the hoop clean over the net. The opposite player is waiting with his stick poised forward, and when the hoop arrives he stabs the stick through it and so prevents it dropping to the ground. The server will have made his throw from the rear line of his court; the one receiving the service will have been standing anywhere in the back half of his court. As soon as the catch is made the hoop can be flung back again – and so the game goes on until one or the other makes a fault, or misses the hoop.

It is a fault for the hoop to drop anywhere outside the court, or in the section nearest to the net, or in fact for the hoop to touch the ground anywhere. But similarly it is a fault if a player, having safely received the hoop on his stick, allows it to slide down and touch his hand or any part of his body. The checking of the swift glide of the hoop on the stick, by a dropping back of the stick's point, is a matter that needs considerable practice.

The general Net Game Rules in *Chapter 5* are applicable to the game in all matters of scoring, serving, and so on.

Sword tennis is not a fiercely competitive game, though of course each player is concerned to make the hoop drop in such a part of the court and in such a manner that his companion cannot retrieve it. At the same time, there is unusual scope for agility and neat footwork – the dexterity of a fencer. The sheer artistry of the game makes it very attractive.

Be particularly careful to enforce the rule that every throw must be made with an upward tendency. The purpose of restricting play to the rear parts of the courts is simply to make impossible a sharp downward fling of the hoop which would render impossible any catching. Anything like a tennis or badminton 'kill' is out of the question by the very nature of the game.

25 TOE BALL

This is an amusing little game, which involves quite considerable energy. Two players can have much fun from it, though any number may take part.

The equipment needed is trifling. A large ball of fair weight, with a piece of cord a couple of feet long, and at the end of the cord a loop – that is all.

All you have to do is to lie on the lawn on your back, with legs straight. The loop of cord is put over the toe of one shoe, and the ball placed in line so that the cord is at full stretch, as far from your foot as it will go. Then, you kick the straight leg upwards with all your vigour, so that the ball is flung upwards and backwards over your head. As it flies the loop naturally slips from your toe and the ball travels free through the air, with the string trailing after it.

Then your companion has a turn. The winner is the person who can fling the ball farthest. Measurements are made in a straight line with the body to the point at which the ball touches ground.

This is an excellent little stunt for the lawn when you are sun-bathing in swim suits.

CHAPTER TWO

GAMES FOR
SMALL GROUPS

26 BADMINTON

The size and measurements of badminton courts are shown in the accompanying diagrams. Heavy outdoor shuttles should be used for garden play. On a day when there is no wind there are few games to equal badminton. One feature that often gives it an advantage is the comparatively small size of the playing area – badminton often fits on a lawn where tennis is impracticable. The badminton net is 5 ft. high.

You may play your game by freely adapting the simple Net Game Rules in *Chapter 5*, or you may go by the official laws.

It is outside the scope of this book to give the full official code, but here are some of the outstanding rules if you would begin to play the proper game. They are numbered as in the 'Laws of Badminton,' and are reprinted by kind permission of the *Badminton Association*.

The Four-Handed or Doubles Game

6. *The Choice of Courts.* – The side winning the toss shall have the first choice of – (a) Serving first; (b) Not serving first; (c) Ends. The side losing the toss shall then have choice of any alternative remaining. The side winning the game shall always serve first in the next game, but in doubles either of the winners may continue serving and either of the losers may receive the service.

7. The four-handed game consists of 15 or 21 aces, as may be arranged. Provided that in a game of 15 aces, where the score is

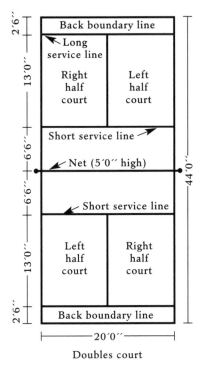

Doubles court

13 all, the side which first reached 13 has the option of 'setting' the game to 5, and that when the score is 14 all, the side which first reached 14 has the option of 'setting' the game to 3. After a game has been 'set' the score is called 'love all,' and the side which first scores 5 or 3 aces, according as the game has been 'set' at 13 or 14 all, wins the game. In either case the claim to 'set' the game must be made before the next service is delivered after the score has reached 13 all or 14 all. Providing also that in a game of 21 aces the same method of scoring be adopted, substituting 19 and 20 for 13 and 14.

8. A rubber is the best of three games. The players shall change ends at the commencement of the second game, and also of the

third game, if a third game is necessary to decide the rubber. In the third game the players shall also change ends, when the leading score reaches 8 in a game of 15 aces, or 11 in a game of 21 aces....

Faults

10. It is a fault:

(a) If the service is overhand ... if the shuttle at the instant of being struck be higher than the server's waist ...

(b) If, in serving, the shuttle falls into the wrong half court (*i.e.* into the one not diagonally opposite to the server), or falls short of the short service line, or beyond the long service line or outside the side boundary lines of the half court into which the service is in order.

(c) If the server's feet are not in the half court in which service is at the time being in order, or if the feet of the player taking the service are not in the half court into which service is at the time being in order ... until the service is delivered. (A foot on the line is out of court.)

The Play

11. It having been decided which side is to have the first service, the player in the right-hand half court of that side commences the game by serving to the player in the opposite right-hand half court. If the latter player returns the shuttle before it touches the ground, it is to be returned by one of the 'in' side, and then returned by one of the 'out' side, and so on, till a fault is made or the shuttle ceases to be 'in play.' If a fault is made by the 'in' side, the server's hand is out, and as the side beginning the game has only one hand in its first innings (*vide* Law 14), the player in the right-hand opposite half court now becomes the server, but if the service is not returned, or the fault is made by the 'out' side, the 'in' side scores an ace. The 'in' side players then change from one half court to the other, the server now being in the left-hand half court. So long as a side remains 'in' service is delivered alternately

from each half court into the one diagonally opposite, the change being made by the 'in' side when, and only when, an ace is added to its score. The first service of a side in each innings shall be made from the right-hand half court. After the service is delivered, the server and the player served to may take up any positions they choose on their side of the net, irrespective of any boundary lines.

General Rules

14. The side beginning a game has only one hand in its first innings. In all subsequent innings each partner on each side has a hand, the partners serving consecutively.

16. It is a 'let' if the shuttle touches the net in service, providing the service be otherwise good, but if in play it does not invalidate the stroke...

The Two-Handed or Singles Game

20. In games of one player on each side the above rules hold good, except that:

(a) The players shall serve from and receive service in the right-hand half courts only when the server's score is 0, or when he has scored an even number of aces in the game, the service being

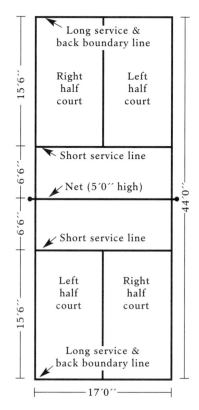

Long service & back boundary line

Right half court | Left half court

15′6″

Short service line

Net (5′0″ high)

6′6″

6′6″

Short service line

Left half court | Right half court

15′6″

Long service & back boundary line

44′0″

17′0″

delivered from and served in the left-hand half courts when the server has scored an odd number of aces.

(b) Both players shall change half courts after each ace has been scored, and consecutive services shall be received by the same player.

27 BULLBOARD

This popular shipboard game is equally suitable for the lawn. Discs and board are all that are needed.

The board is set up and the players take their stand at the throwing line – usually 6 ft. for ladies and 9 ft. for men.

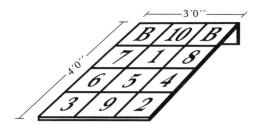

Each player in turn takes the six discs and, standing at the line, endeavours to throw them one at a time upon the divisions marked on the board, in the following order:

(a) Numbers 1 to 10 consecutively,

(b) The right-hand Bull square (that is, the square with a bull's head or a letter B marked in it),

(c) The left-hand Bull square;

Then, reversing the order,

(d) The left-hand Bull square,

(e) The right-hand Bull square,

(f) Numbers 10 to 1 consecutively.

At the end of a player's turn the last division he has attained in the correct order is noted, and the next player goes on to throw the discs.

Any disc touching a line does not score. But as the discs lie upon the board until the player's turn is completed, one disc may drive another from a line completely into a division, and thus score.

When a disc falls off the board the player's score is reckoned back one division. If one of the Bull squares is scored out of its correct order the player must recommence altogether.

That player wins who first accomplishes the full round and returns to No. 1 in the correct order.

It is unlikely that you will desire to make your own bull-board equipment, but if you should the board measurements should be 4 ft. by 3 ft., so that squares each measure 12 in. The canvas-covered or rubber discs should be about 3 in. across.

28 CIRCLE BADMINTON

The 'field' of play can be 5 to 15 yds. across, and has the novel feature of being circular in form. If the larger size is practicable in your garden, then doubles can be played; if you have little space, then only two players should take part.

A peg or short post is driven into the middle of the lawn and to this a string is attached, with a shuttle fastened to the end – the string will give you the radius of the circle in which play takes place. Across the circle, running through the centre, is a straight line; this marks the two halves.

Play proceeds in the manner of ordinary net games, as far as possible, a point being lost every time the shuttle touches the ground or becomes entangled in a racket.

All strokes must be played upwards; a point is forfeited if an overhead or downward stroke is made.

Padders can be used for this game, instead of badminton rackets; they are even advisable if the playing circle is very small. How to make a padder is described in the last chapter of this book.

29 CIRCLE BALL

This is exactly the same as the preceding game, except that a tennis ball is used instead of a shuttle. The manner of tethering a ball is dealt with in *Chapter 5*, along with the making of padders.

Tennis rackets or padders may be used.

After a little practice it will be found that the tethering string is very little hindrance to free play, and need hardly ever become entangled in a racket. The slight drag that it causes necessitates harder hitting – which compensates for the comparatively small court.

30 CROQUET

This ever popular game can be adapted for almost any lawn. The diagram here shows the hoop arrangements for wide or narrow courts.

Though it is impossible to give here the full official rules, the following simple synopsis, reprinted by kind permission of the Croquet Association, is adequate for a sound preliminary understanding of the game:

Croquet is played with four balls, Blue and Black v. Red and Yellow. In starting the game each ball plays in turn from one of the two inner lines termed baulks. Thereafter the sides, but not necessarily the colours of that side, play alternately.

Both balls of a side must score all points to win. A ball propelled through its hoop by the action of another ball may score the point.

The four outside hoops (No. 1 having a blue cross-bar) are first scored, then 5 and 6 in the centre. They are subsequently scored the reverse way, from the 2nd, which becomes 1 back, to the 6th (now called the penultimate), then the Rover (with red cross-bar), and finally the winning peg is hit. The coloured clips indicate the objective hoop, and are placed on the crown for 1 to 6 and on the upright for 1 back to rover.

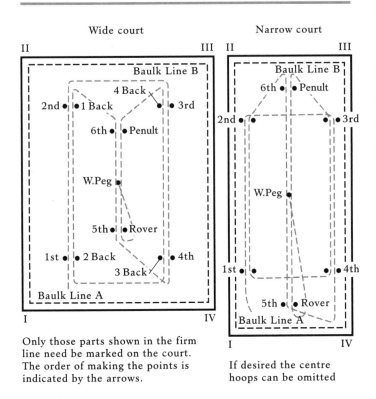

Wide court

Narrow court

Only those parts shown in the firm line need be marked on the court. The order of making the points is indicated by the arrows.

If desired the centre hoops can be omitted

A turn is a stroke or series of strokes, extra ones being earned by:

(1) Hitting another ball with your own ball (making a 'roquet'). The two balls are then placed in contact, the player 'takes off' (takes 'croquet') from the other ball and is then entitled to make a further stroke.

(2) Passing through (running) a hoop.

The player may take croquet from each ball once during his turn, but may not do so a second time in the same turn unless meantime he has run a hoop. By a combination of taking croquet and running hoops, several or all the hoops can be scored by the player in one turn. This is called 'making a break.' In a four-ball break three other balls are used. In a three-ball break two of them. In a two-ball break, one.

It will be apparent that the player wishes to use or control as many balls as possible himself, and to prevent the opponent from doing so. For these reasons most players start by going to a corner, or side boundary, as the fourth ball to start is the only one that really has a chance of an immediate break. The second player often plays his ball about 7 yards out from a baulk, hoping the third will shoot at it (and miss!) instead of joining the partner. The third player frequently takes this shot, as, should he hit, he can lay the balls in such a manner as to give him the chance of a break, should the fourth ball fail to hit. During a game, if a break is not feasible, players sometimes elect to go to a corner or boundary to make the opponent's turn more difficult.

A turn is concluded when the player has made all the strokes to which he is entitled, or if he fails to make a roquet, or run a hoop, or if when taking croquet he sends either ball over the boundary. The turn also ceases if the player makes an illegal stroke or 'foul' as defined in the Laws.

31 FISHING

Four or six players can take part in this amusing game. The equipment is not difficult to prepare. First, about a couple of dozen cotton reels. To the end of each of these fasten a loop of string, or drive in an iron staple. Then get the fish. These are cut-out paper shapes about 2 to 4 inches long. On each paper fish is written a weight. With two dozen fish the weights may be apportioned thus: three 1 oz., three 2 oz., three 4 oz., two 8 oz., two 1 lb., two 2 lb., three 3 lb., three 4 lb., three 5 lb.

These paper fish are coiled up and each tucked into a cotton-reel hole.

Only 'fishing rods' are now needed, one for each player. A rod consists simply of a cane or stick 4 to 5 ft. long. To the end of this is a string of about the same length, and to the end of the string a wire or metal hook is fastened.

Now the game can begin. Stand up your reels in a marked 'fishpond' on your lawn, and have the players around it. At the starting signal they begin fishing, each trying to get his hook in the loop of a reel. No one can tell, of course, what weight the fish he is landing will be, until he pulls out the paper and reads what he has caught.

So the competitors go on catching one reel after another until none is left in the pond. At the end the total weights caught are reckoned, and the player with the heaviest catch is the winner.

It does not matter whether players look to see the weight of their catches as they go along, or leave the discovery till all have finished. It is hard to resist looking each time a fish is landed.

32 GLORIA

Four players take part in this. Each is equipped with a short stick, and each pair of players have a small wood ring or hoop between them. The four stand at the corners of a square measuring about 5 yds. across, and partners must be at diagonally opposite corners.

The game consists in players throwing the rings to their partners. These partners catch the rings on their sticks; for every failure to catch, a point is lost. Each player must make eight throws, and receive eight, in each of three sets.

For the first set the ring is tossed in straightforward fashion, the partners facing each other. First one player gives his eight throws; then his opponent does the same; then the first player in turn receives eight from his partner; and lastly the opponent similarly receives eight.

In the second set, the one who is to receive the ring on his stick must turn round while the ring is in the air; he can spin either to right or left, but of course is back facing his partner when he attempts to make the actual catch.

For the third set the thrower must stand with his back to

his partner and throw the ring over his head.

No player at any time is allowed to step within the square.

33 GOLF-CROQUET

Golf-croquet is an interesting variation of croquet. The rules, by kind permission of the Croquet Association, are here reprinted:

1. The Game
The game of golf-croquet is played between two sides playing alternate turns, each side consisting either of one or two players. The court and setting of the hoops and pegs are the same as in the game of Croquet (see diagram on page 46 but balls are played throughout in the sequence, blue, red, black and yellow – one side playing blue and black, and the other red and yellow.

The game consists of 13 points. The points are scored in the same order as in croquet (game No. 30). The first ball to make a point scores that point for its side. The next point in order is then contested.

2. The Start
The choice of start or the allocation of balls is decided as in croquet. At the commencement of the game each player, in due sequence, shall play his ball from any spot on the east yard line.

3. The Turn
The turn shall consist of a single stroke, even though the striker hit another ball or make a point-in-order. There is no croquet-stroke in golf-croquet.

4. Method of Scoring
The state of the game is indicated as in match play in golf. As in golf it will not be necessary to complete the whole series of points to win the game if either side has scored a balance of points greater in number than remain to be played.

5. Playing at Peg

After the rover hoop has been scored, each ball (whatever its position may be) shall, until the end of the game and *immediately* before its turn, be lifted to any point on the yard-line and played therefrom.

6. Peeling

If a striker's ball hits another ball and causes it to run a hoop in order or hit the peg in order, then that other ball scores the point in order.

7. Advancing a Ball Prematurely for the Next Point

If the striker plays his ball, without hitting another ball to a position which commands or threatens to command the point succeeding that which is being contested, the adversary may require such ball to be replaced and the stroke shall be made again to the adversary's satisfaction; but, if the striker hits another ball or scores a point, no ball displaced by the stroke can be so recalled.

8. Fouls

Strokes which are fouls in croquet are fouls in golf-croquet, and the penalties ... are the same.

9. Jump-Stroke

The jump-stroke is a foul in golf-croquet.

10. Playing Out of Turn or with a Wrong Ball

If the striker plays out of turn or with a wrong ball, that stroke and any subsequent strokes are null and void. All balls displaced shall be replaced; the right ball shall be played by the correct player, and the other balls shall follow in due sequence. No points made during the period of error shall be scored.

If the players cannot mutually agree as to the original position of the balls, all balls shall be lifted and played from the corner square nearest to the point being contested; but the player first in error shall play last in sequence.

34 HANDBALL

This excellent game necessitates that the playing court shall butt against a high wall – perhaps the end of a house. The diagram given sets out the measurements in vogue for a 'hard' court of concrete or something similar. If you desire to play on grass, it will probably be desirable to reduce the court size; because the ball will not bounce so readily.

The game consists of knocking the ball against the wall with the flat hand so that it bounces back into the rear half of the court. Two or four players take part. To begin, one bounces the ball behind the service line and knocks it against the back wall. The opponent, when the ball rebounds into the rear half, may either let it bounce once on the ground before playing it or may volley it. After that the first player takes the rebound – and so on. Each side, or individual player in singles, must strike the ball in turn, until a fault is made and a point lost. Naturally, each tries to

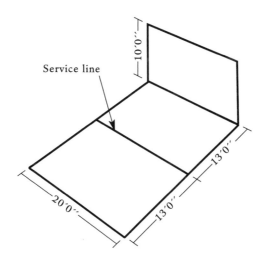

Service line

make the ball come back in such a fashion that the succeeding player cannot play it. When a fault occurs on the part of the one who serves, his opponent instead of counting a point takes over the service – in the same way as is described in the Net Game Rules in *Chapter 5*. Thus only the player who has served can score.

Points are scored, or the service changes over, whenever any of these things happen:

1. When the two services allowed are both faults – that is, do not strike the back wall properly and rebound into the rear court;
2. When the ball hits the wall outside the boundary lines;
3. When the ball touches the ground outside the rear court;
4. When the ball bounces more than once;
5. When the ball is struck before it has come over the service line;
6. When a player, serving, steps outside the rear court;
7. When the ball, being served, comes back and strikes the server or his partner;
8. When the ball is struck more than once in an attempt to serve or return it.

In doubles partners take it in turn to serve. In singles the same player serves until he loses the service. The game is won by the first side to get 21 points.

Use a tennis ball, and wear gloves if you like.

35 HOOP BOWLS

A row of six croquet hoops are set up in line, side by side, but with enough space between for a croquet ball to pass through. Players then stand at a bowling line perhaps 5 yds. away, and each in turn bowls up one croquet ball.

The aim of the players is to get through every hoop in turn in proper order, and the first to achieve this wins the game. Thus a player must keep aiming at the first hoop until he gets through, even though he has a dozen turns before he is able to pass on to the second hoop.

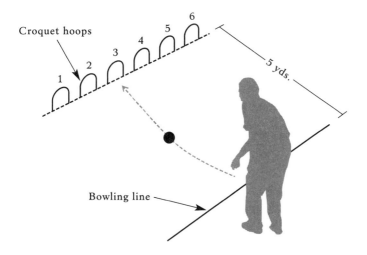

It is helpful to have a person standing behind the hoops who will send the balls back.

36 HOOP TENNIS

An ordinary tennis net, or a net of tennis height, $3\frac{1}{2}$ ft., is needed for this. Above the middle of it is suspended a wooden hoop of moderate size. A string across the court from two posts about 6 ft. high can support the top edge of the hoop and the lower edge can be fastened to the middle of the net. Probably a couple of fastenings will be needed at the top, to prevent the hoop twisting – it must stay flatly in line with the net all the time.

Play now goes on as in ordinary tennis, except that the chief aim is to drive the ball through the hoop.

There should be a line across the court, parallel with the net and about 3 yds. from it. The purpose of this is to prevent players standing close to the hoop and merely volleying back any balls that come through. All other play can be as close to the net as in an ordinary game, but no ball must be driven through the hoop from any point in front of this line.

Ordinary tennis scoring is used, or the Net Game Rules in *Chapter 5* can be substituted. But always there is an extra point counted when a ball goes through the hoop.

The size of the hoop can be varied according to skill and preference. Similarly, the court can be of tennis dimensions, or as much smaller as circumstances make necessary.

37 HORSESHOE RINGING

This is a form of quoits played with horseshoes. Four shoes are required. They should be fairly light, and the points should be knocked down so that they do not tear the turf. The peg used must be of iron, and should stand 8 in. out of the ground – the manner of fixing a socket so that the peg can be slipped in or out when desired is described in the last chapter of this book.

A 'rink' of standard length as used in America, where the game is popular, measures 40 ft., but if you have to be content with something less you may still have excellent play. Either one or two pegs may be employed. If one, the throwing line will be marked on the ground at the proper distance; if two, a 3-ft. circle is marked round each peg, and throwers must stand within the circle. With the two pegs, of course, one is at each end of the rink, so that opponents stand at opposite ends and receive each other's horseshoes, instead of having to walk up to recover them from the single peg.

Two or four players take part, and the four shoes are divided between them. The opposing sides take alternate throws, until the four shoes have been flung – then the score is reckoned.

Round the peg a circle of 8 in. radius will have been marked, and this will help to determine the points gained. The scores are as follows:

3 points when the peg is 'ringed.'

1 point for any shoe inside the 8-in, circle.

1 additional point to the shoe inside the circle which is nearest to the peg.

The first player or side to get 21 points wins.

Much of the art of throwing horseshoes depends on giving the right amount of spin so that the shoe arrives at the peg with open end forward – otherwise it cannot become a 'ringer.' If shoes are displaced by succeeding throws that does not matter – only their final lie determines their score.

38 LADDER GOLF

Mark out the ladder on your lawn, 30 to 50 ft. long, and about 3 ft. wide; the rungs will be 3 to 5 ft. wide. Number your ten rungs, 1 to 10, and sink a golf hole beyond the tenth rung. The making of the hole is described in *Chapter 5*.

Ordinary golf irons and balls are used. The game consists of driving the ball up the ladder and into the hole from every rung in turn, beginning with the first. Supposing there are two players – each can play the whole ladder straight off, or each can do one rung at a time, the winner being he who gets the lowest total number of strokes for the full ladder.

Alternatively, players can compete for each rung in turn, so that the winner is the one who wins most rungs.

A ball going over the side of the ladder must be replaced at that point on the line where it went out, and this replacing counts as one stroke.

Players should stand outside the ladder as much as possible.

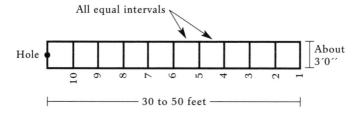

39 LAWN BILLIARDS

The equipment for this novel game can be procured through a sports dealer – or you may make your own. For cues you need poles, like broom-handles. To the end of each a stiff wire or iron ring about 3 in. in diameter is attached. This ring must be flat and in line with the handle so that it can be pushed under a ball by the player holding the pole.

The billiard 'table' is a flat piece of lawn measuring 12 yds. by 6 yds., or some smaller size. The 'pockets' are at the middle of the table – four croquet hoops placed in the form of a square, close together, so that one hoop faces each side and end of the 'table,' or field of play.

Two or four players take part, and four balls are in play, each of a different colour.

Opening shots are made from the bottom end of the 'table,' each player in turn playing his ball up to the centre. After that balls remain in play, and only those that are 'pocketed' come down for a restart. To play a ball the player stands behind it and thrusts the ring at the end of the cue under it; then, holding the cue firmly in both hands, he half thrusts and half flings the ball forward – so that it rises only a few inches from the lawn, if at all.

One point is counted when a ball goes through a hoop; one point if a ball cannons, or strikes any two other balls in succession from the same stroke; and two points if a ball first strikes another ball and then goes through a hoop – an 'in off' shot. Balls passing

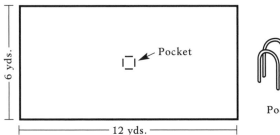

Pocket

over the outer boundaries are replaced at that point on the line where they go out. A player continues in play as long as he is scoring, ceasing when his 'break' finishes. No points are lost for shots that are missed. *Game* can be 50 or 100 points.

40 LAWN TENNIS

It is superfluous to give here details of play or rules for this most popular of garden games – there are few in these days who do not know how to play. But it may be useful to indicate the markings and measurements of a court.

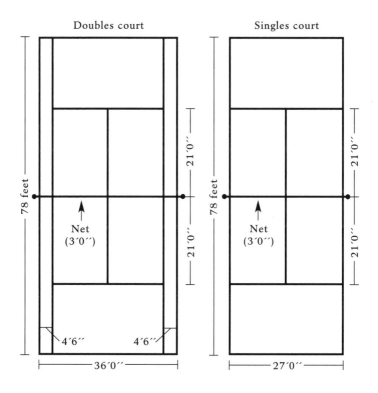

Doubles court   Singles court

78 feet

21′0′′

21′0′′

Net (3′0′′)

4′6′′   4′6′′

36′0′′

27′0′′

CHAPTER TWO

41 NET HOOPLA

The court and general rules of play may be such as described in *Chapter 5*, but have the court on each side of the net divided by a transverse line into front and rear halves – all throws must be taken from the rear halves.

A large, light wooden hoop is required. Two or four players may take part; the best game is with doubles.

The game consists in throwing the hoop backwards and forwards over the net, keeping it flat all the time. Players try to get into such positions that they are 'ringed,' the hoop dropping over them.

Service is taken from any part of the rear half of each court, the hoop of course being tossed in an upward direction – for the net must be 6 ft. high. The player receiving the service aims at getting in such a position that, with arms raised above his head, he may let the hoop fall cleanly down over him – unless he succeeds in being ringed he loses a point. But if he is successful then he tosses the hoop back from his own rear court.

It is worth-while rubbing the sharp edges from the hoop with some glasspaper.

42 PADDER TENNIS

Padders can readily be bought, or quite easily made – as shown in the last chapter of the book.

Padder tennis is a miniature lawn tennis, and possesses most of the fine qualities of the better-known game. Every stroke and bit of strategy is the same – the main difference is in the size of the court – the padder court is half as long and half as wide as the lawn tennis court. It is thus practicable to split up one ordinary court into four padder courts.

The net used is only 2 ft. high, and the balls are of sponge rubber. This latter fact, combined with the fact that the padders are of solid wood, reduces the flight of the balls in just sufficient degree that strokes can be made with exactly the same vigour and strength as in ordinary tennis conditions – and the ball will travel only half as far.

It is advisable to take over lawn tennis scoring and rules exactly; but if preferred the Net Game Rules in the last chapter will serve quite adequately.

43 PEG POOL

A post or peg about 15 in. high is fitted into the end of the lawn – the method of making such peg and socket, which can be utilized for various other games, is described in *Chapter 5*. Round this peg mark a circle with a diameter of about 12 in., and on top of the peg place a stone.

The players are provided with throwing sticks – about 15 in. long and ½ in. thick is a good size – and from a line 5 to 10 yds. away throws are made at the peg.

One point is scored each time the stone is knocked from the top of the peg, so that it falls outside the marked circle. When the stone falls inside the circle there is no score. The first player or side to get 21 points wins.

It will be found that only direct hits are likely to drive the stone outside the ring.

44 RING TENNIS

This is the finest of garden games; it is equal in every respect, for enjoyment value and skill, to lawn tennis itself. The game goes under a great many names – *ring tennis, deck tennis, quoit tennis, ship tennis, tenikoit*. To be played under ideal conditions the court should be as described in *Chapter 5*, and the Net Game Rules given in the same chapter are adequate. While it is possible to play on the tiny court which often has to serve on board ship, the full 40 ft. by 18 ft. is much better; and similarly, though a rope quoit ring can be made to do, it is far better to have a sponge rubber tenikoit ring – any sports dealer can supply this.

The net must be 5 ft. high, it does not much matter how low it hangs. The usual tenikoit net is a couple of feet deep and is made very strongly to withstand the considerable strain imposed on it in a hard game.

The ring must always be upright during play, not flat or horizontal; and every throw must be an upward direction – rather like the action of underarm bowling. Overhead or downward throws are not allowed. Because of the upright position of the ring, which makes throwing and catching easy, the ring generally has a spinning motion while in flight, and this helps to steady it. 'Wobbling' rings are not permissible.

A point is lost each time the ring touches the ground. It must be caught, and returned immediately from the point where it was caught. All catching and throwing must be done by a single hand; it is a fault to touch the ring with two hands simultaneously, and a point is forfeited.

45 SLAB TENNIS

The same court and Net Game Rules described in the last chapter of the book serve for this game also, which resembles *padder tennis*, though now the net is 4 ft. high.

It is not difficult to make your own *slabs*. Each consists of a circular piece of wood about ½ in. thick and 9 in. across. To the back of this a piece of strap or webbing is fastened at both ends, thus forming a loose band under which the flat hand can slide. With the palm of the hand thus pressed against the back of the slab, and the band holding the back of the hand firmly, the slab can be used freely to knock the sponge rubber ball across the net.

From a sports dealer you may obtain a *miniten* 'thug,' which is a sort of double slab between which the hand slips and which therefore allows backhand as well as forehand strokes to be played.

Slab tennis can be very fast as rallies consist very often of a series of volleys.

46 SPIRAL GOLF

Clock golf equipment is needed for this (No. 56). The manner of making a hole is described in *Chapter 5*.

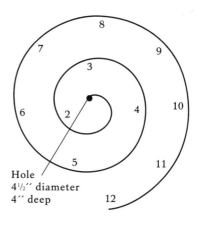

Hole
4½″ diameter
4″ deep

The game is an interesting variation of clock golf as it allows each succeeding number to be played from an increased distance, instead of all from the circumference of the same circle.

It is advisable to mark out the spiral with chalk or whitening, or with a tape line, and then to fix the numbers at evenly spaced intervals. The longer the putts the better the game.

Players can play the whole round, determining the winner by the total strokes required to hole the ball from every number in turn. Or each number may be competed for separately, that player or side winning which wins the most holes.

Of course there is no need to get clock golf equipment, other than the numbers, if you have the real thing – golf irons and balls.

47 TETHER BADMINTON

In many gardens it is impracticable to play many net games because of the proximity of neighbouring gardens, and the inconvenience of having safeguarding high nets around the courts. In such circumstances a tethered game like this is most useful, for if the shuttle does happen to go out of bounds it can promptly be hauled back by its string.

Mark out your court and play according to the usage of ordinary badminton, or the Net Game Rules given in *Chapter 5*.

The tethering string must be fastened round the base of the shuttle and to the top edge of the net, at the middle, and must be long enough to allow the shuttle to reach the corners of the court.

Ordinary badminton rackets are used, and the play goes on in straightforward fashion. The string, it will be found, hampers the shuttle much less than might be expected, though it naturally necessitates harder hitting. A point is forfeited when a racket or a player becomes entangled in the string.

48 TETHER TENNIS

This game bears the same relation to lawn tennis that the preceding game, tether badminton, does to ordinary badminton. It is simply ordinary tennis with a tethered ball – the method of fastening string to ball is described in the last chapter of the book.

It is advisable to have the court considerably smaller than for the standard game, and the measurements given in *Chapter 5* are very suitable.

Because of the slight hindrance in the bouncing qualities of the ball there is a good deal of volleying.

49 THREE-COURT BALL

This is a fine game which requires almost no equipment. A large ball that bounces well – possibly one of the familiar reinforced rubber bladders, and a court marked as the following diagram, that is all:

The two end courts and the middle or neutral area are all of the same size; the total length may be 15 yds. Width can be determined in part by the number of players – 3 or 4 a side makes an ideal arrangement.

The neutral area serves as a net, for across it the ball must be patted or punched. Neither player nor ball must touch the middle court. Neither must the ball touch the ground in either end court. Thus a point is lost every time the ball touches the

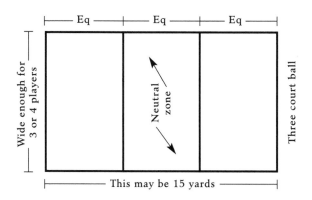

ground, no matter where. A player stepping into the dead court also loses a point for his side.

The general Net Game Rules in the last chapter of the book can, in the main, apply to three-court ball. Naturally if the ball falls outside the proper court that team which last touched the ball loses the point; but if it falls within the proper court it is the receiving side which is at fault and forfeits the point.

More than one player on the same side can handle the ball before it is returned to the opponents. No holding or carrying is allowed – only striking with palm or fist.

50 ZIGZAG CROQUET

Place a row of croquet hoops down the middle of your lawn, side by side. On either side of this row mark a straight line, 3 ft. out from the hoops. You will thus have two straight and parallel lines, 6 ft. apart, and the row of hoops, evenly spaced out, down the middle of this avenue.

The game consists of driving croquet balls backwards and forwards across this avenue and through one hoop after of another. Thus a zigzag progress is achieved down the entire line of hoops.

No ball, unless it is outside the lines, can be played at any

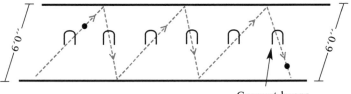

Croquet hoops

hoop. If a ball lies within the lines, it must first be played the outwards, and only then can it be driven back to its next hoop.

The players taking part should have only one stroke each at a time, so that they may possibly dislodge or hamper their opponents' balls as the course is traversed. It is permissible to play at an opponent instead of at a hoop, if desired.

That player wins who first gets his ball through every hoop. But every hoop must be played from its proper side. In order to show which must be gone through from the front and which from the back, it is advisable to tie a piece of tape on each second hoop.

CHAPTER THREE

GAMES FOR LARGER PARTIES

51 BALLOON GOAL

This is an odd-moment frolic more than a serious game. Any number can take part, but it is best to work it off two at a time, the winner of each pair taking on the next comer.

All that you need is a goal at each end of your lawn, or about 10 to 20 yds. apart. A couple of sticks a yard apart from each other form a goal. A balloon is needed – and a few in reserve – and folded newspapers, or fans, or wooden padders for the players.

To start the game the balloon is placed at the centre, and then the players begin to waft it along with their papers or whatever they may have. No touching is permitted, the balloon must only be propelled by the windy gusts. The first player to get the balloon through his opponent's goal wins the bout, and takes on the next contestant.

52 BEANBAG

This is one of the pleasantest forms of non-strenuous throwing games.

Beanbags can be bought, or made as described in *Chapter 5*. A dozen of them are desirable, but the game can be played with fewer. The board, which lies flat on the ground with its back edge raised about six inches, consists usually of a piece of three-ply wood measuring 2 ft. across and 3 ft. from back to front. Two holes are cut in this, each measuring 6 in. across. The front hole is square, and the other, lying behind it, is round, and so smaller.

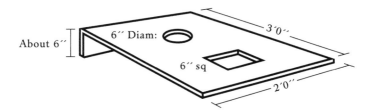

Players stand about 5 yds. from the board, and each in turn tosses up all the beanbags, from the flat palm of the hand. Only the final lie of the bags matters – a bag, for instance, knocked off the board by a succeeding throw loses the points which otherwise it would have secured. The scores are as follows:

15 points for a bag which drops through the round hole.
10 points for a bag which drops through the square hole.
5 points for a bag which remains on the board.

It is permissible to remove bags that have fallen through the holes, particularly through the square hole, so that they do not obstruct the hole, as they easily can do if they pile on each other.

When there is a question as to whether a bag is on or off the board, the point must be decided by gently lifting the board – if the bag does not drop off it is then counted as on.

53 BEANBAG DUCKSTONE

Six to ten players can take part in this game, which affords plenty of excitement and continuous occupation for everyone.

A big flowerpot, upside down, forms a very good duckstone, or alternatively a quoit peg as described in *Chapter 5* will serve, though the beanbag is apt to catch on this. Each player is provided with a beanbag – the making of which is also dealt with in the last chapter of the book.

Around the duckstone a ring of 5 ft. radius is marked, and 20 ft. away is the throwing line. One player places his bag on the duckstone and stands near to it; the rest line up at the throwing line. Their purpose is to get as many throws as they can, trying each time to knock the beanbag from the duckstone.

Each player throws in turn, and then runs up to recover his bag. But if he steps within the circle and is tagged by the guardian there the two change places, and as tossed bags generally do fall within the circle there is small chance of recovering a bag unless the guardian is momentarily out of action. He can be put out of action by knocking his bag from the duckstone, for whenever that happens he cannot tag anyone until the bag is replaced. This gives waiting players an opportunity to grab their bags, and get back to the throwing line. And as there is generally someone at the line

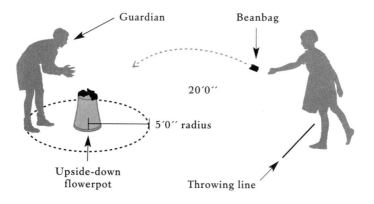

Guardian   Beanbag

20′0″

5′0″ radius

Upside-down
flowerpot

Throwing line

throwing the players around the circle do not have to wait long before their chance comes.

When a player is tagged and becomes guardian of the duckstone all the others return to the throwing line for a new start.

54 BOCCI

This old Mediterranean game (pronounced *botchee*) is a simple form of bowls, most suitable for the garden because it allows almost any balls that are available to be utilized. Each of two teams, for instance, can be provided with nine balls – three croquet, three tennis, three golf. In addition one other small ball, the *lick* – serving as the *jack* in bowls, is needed.

The team leaders toss. The winner throws the lick up the lawn; then they each roll up one ball. The one who gets nearest to the lick is entitled to start the game.

The starting team sends up its nine balls – unless they prefer to make their opponents begin. Then the other side follows on. When all the balls are gone the team with the ball nearest to the lick counts one point for each of its balls which is closer to the lick than the best of the opponents' balls.

At the restart the team which previously bowled second will go first. The first team to get 21 points wins the game.

Obviously it will be an advantage for one set of balls to be distinctly coloured or marked. Red ink or dye will colour them.

55 BOWLS

It is unnecessary to deal with the technique and official rules of this popular game in a general book of this nature. But it is appropriate to point out that *garden bowls* sets are obtainable, which are intended to be used on lawns that are not perfect, in the bowls sense. Thus cheaper woods are made, and though the game is played under ordinary bowls rules a rather easier standard of play is necessarily expected.

A mat is placed on which one foot of the bowler must rest entirely when a bowl is being delivered. The first player sends the *jack* up the lawn. Following this each player in singles sends up four bowls; with four players, each will send up two.

Players bowl alternately, and when all the bowls are up the 'end' is won by that player who has more bowls nearer to the jack than his opponent. It is usual to agree beforehand on how many ends shall be played – often it is 12 ends, or an hour's play. The winner, of the course, will be the one who secures most ends.

56 CLOCK GOLF

This popular game can be played on almost any lawn that is reasonably smooth – whether it is level does not greatly matter. All that is required is sufficient space to describe the circle which forms the clock face. This circle is marked out, preferably in white, with the help of centre peg, string, brush, and whitening, and may be of any convenient size that the lawn will admit; a circle with a diameter of 30 to 40 ft. is most suitable; having marked the circle, divide it into twelve equal parts, placing a mark on the circle line at these spots, which are called the figure points. To complete the clock face the figures are pressed into place at these various points, outside the circle. Lastly, a 'putting' hole is made in the ground at any spot between the centre of the circle and the circumference – by not having it at the centre you ensure that the distance from the various figure points is different. The manner of making a hole is described in *Chapter 5*, and if you already have your golf irons and balls this will be helpful; but if you buy your clock golf outfit complete, then the hole fitting will be included.

The object of the player is to get his ball in the hole from each successive figure point in order, commencing with figure 1, in fewest strokes. One ball and one putter are actually all that the game requires.

That player playing the round of the clock in the least number of strokes wins the game. Alternatively, the game can be decided by holes, each hole in turn being won by that player who holes out in the fewest strokes, and the game is gained by the player who wins the greatest number of holes.

When a number of persons desire to play, sides may be chosen, or play may be by individuals.

Whenever the ball is struck so as to move appreciably from its position the stroke must be counted.

The circle line forms the boundary, and whenever a ball crosses this it must be brought back and played from the point where it went out, one stroke being counted as a penalty. In general, ordinary golf rules, when applicable, apply to clock golf also.

57 CORNER BALL

The 'field' for this should not be more than 25 yds. long and 15 yds. wide, and may be considerably smaller. It must be clearly marked out as a plain rectangle, with a line running transversely across the middle, dividing it into halves. Also, at each corner, must be a small square, measuring 3 ft. across, in which the corner-men stand.

Almost any number of players can take part, providing they have comfortable room to move about. Two teams are chosen, and each team remains in its own half throughout the game – all except four players. Two players from each team stand in the corner squares of the half court occupied by their opponents, and a point is reckoned every time the ball is caught by one of these players.

To begin, the ball is tossed at the centre, and whoever can catches it as it comes down. The object of each team is to get the ball over the heads of the opposing team into the hands of their corner-men. Corner-men are not allowed to step outside their squares; thus they stand always in the rear of their opponents, waiting to receive the tosses of their partners in the other court.

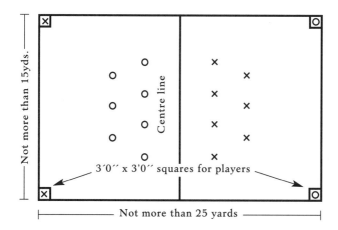

O & X represent the teams

The ball must not be kicked, nor carried. It must be thrown immediately from wherever it happens to be caught. Any number of players in the same team can handle it before throwing across to the corner men.

Game is 5 points, and the first to reach this score wins.

After each point has been scored, by a corner-man getting the ball, the ball must be tossed afresh at the centre – team leaders take it in turns to toss if there is no referee. When the ball goes out of the court it must be thrown in from the point where it crossed the line.

58 END BALL

This game is almost identical with the preceding one, though instead of having merely two corner men in the opponents' court there is a whole line of them right across the rear part of the court. Thus, each team has four or six 'basemen.'

The manner of play is the same as in *corner ball*. But it is a foul for a player to step outside his proper court – the basemen are kept back by a line parallel with the back line of the court and a yard from it. It is a foul also to bounce the ball more than once, or to interfere with an opponent. When a foul is penalized a player from the opposite team is allowed one free throw, which must not be touched by one of the penalized side, though the thrower must throw not to his baseman but to another of his own team before this second passes on to the basemen.

It is, of course, a foul if a baseman steps outside his boundaries.

59 FISHERS' NET

This is best played across a rectangular lawn of fair size. About three players holding hands form the net at the outset, and all the rest run backwards and forwards across the lawn. Those of the net try to catch the rest, and every one caught joins on to the string of those hand-in-hand at the middle.

No one can be captured while the net is broken.

This, of course, is a popular children's game, but it is an excellent thing for family parties in which youngsters as well as grown-ups are taking part.

60 GARDEN SKITTLES

Garden skittles seems always a favourite. Of course it is not strenuous, but it gives plenty of opportunity for real skill. And there are few human beings who do not enjoy knocking things over.

You can spend almost what you like on a garden skittles outfit, and the layout of the skittles when ready for play will depend on their number and size – instructions given with your outfit will tell you about this. The essential thing is that each skittle shall be sufficiently near to its neighbours to make it possible that one of them shall be knocked over also when the first falls. Be sure to have net or board of some sort round the back of the array of pins – as the skittles are usually called.

Of course the pins must stand firmly, and in a good outfit discs which can be placed firmly on the grass are usually supplied; on these discs the pins stand, and can readily be replaced.

The game can be played by any number of players, either singly or as partners.

One form of the game is for the first player to continue to bowl at the pins until he has knocked them all down. Then the second player commences, and if he succeeds in knocking all the pins down with fewer balls than did the other, then he scores one point. The first to get 5 points wins.

In another form each player in turn is allowed to bowl three balls. If all the skittles are knocked down by the first ball, 30 points are scored; if by two, 20 points are scored; and if the third ball is used, one point only is scored for each pin knocked over. The player whose score first totals 50 points is the winner.

All balls should be thrown by an underarm bowling action; they must not be pitched. Should a ball not reach the nearest pin, it may be replayed. If a ball rebounds from the net or back-board upon the skittles and overthrows any of them, it is considered a foul, and the pin is replaced. Any pin overthrown by another pin is, of course, counted as properly scored.

The normal throwing distance for garden skittles is about 10 yds.

61 HORSE RACING

Under such names as *derby*, *race game*, and so on, this form of amusement is as suitable and popular for gardens as for the decks of ships.

In the best games of this sort the race depends entirely on the skill of the players. Two or more persons can take part, and horses attached by means of long cords to winders are drawn along the ground by the winding handles. The drum round which the string winds is cone-shaped, and thus the speed of the horse depends upon the skill of the player in so manipulating his cord that it continues to wind on to the thick part of the spindle.

There is plenty of fun and excitement, for the horses are continually changing positions. Handicaps can be arranged by shortening some of the strings.

The back line of a net game court may form the winning line, over which the horses are to be drawn. If possible, a starter and judge should be appointed.

The players, with their winders of various colours, take up their positions immediately behind the winning line at the end of the course. The horses are carried to the distance available – and the race is started. Each player winds as fast as he can, trying to keep the string in the centre and on the greater diameter of the winding drum. If the string slides down to the narrower part of the spindle the horse's speed is very greatly reduced, but it speeds up as the string climbs back to the centre, though the player needs to be very careful if the string is not to run down the other side. Players should keep their eyes on their winders, not on the horses.

Should a horse fall over during a race, the player must at once cease winding and ask the starter, or an onlooker, to put it on its feet again.

62 HUMAN CROQUET

A large number of people can take part in this amusing game – some are players, others act as balls and hoops.

First the 'hoops' are placed around the field of play. Each hoop consists of two people standing facing each other, with hands clasped and held high in the air so that their arms form an arch under which the 'ball' can pass. Of course, the hoop need not keep their arms up like this except at the moment a ball is passing through.

Each 'ball' is blindfolded, and is guided and directed solely by the player to whom it belongs.

To begin the game, the balls are placed on the starting line and played off one at a time. The player stands behind his ball and gripping his arms points him in then desired direction, at the first hoop, then says 'Go!' On this the ball trots forward and continues until the order 'Stop!' is given. If the blindfold player has passed successfully under the first hoop another stroke is allowed.

As far as possible the rules of ordinary croquet should be applied, and the general directions given in the previous chapter. (No. 30.)

Each player is only allowed to *aim* his ball, and must not afterwards touch or direct him. The first player to negotiate every hoop wins the game.

Take care that each ball passes through hoops from the right direction; any ball overrunning a hoop must of course be brought back in order that it may go through from the proper side.

63 LAWN POOL

The playing court or 'table' should measure something like 10 yds. long and 5 yds. wide, and should be marked out with 'pockets,' like a billiard table, as shown in the diagram:

Any number of players can take part, providing each can have a separate ball; if only a few are playing, the size of the court

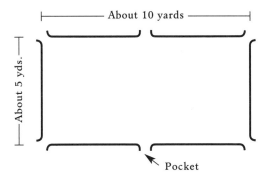

About 10 yards

About 5 yds.

Pocket

can be reduced. All balls must be alike in size and weight, though they should have distinguishing colours. Croquet or skittle balls serve very well; tennis and soft balls are less satisfactory, though they can be used.

The game begins by one player placing his ball in the middle of the court, and the next in turn bowling his at it from the bottom line of the court. The third player must bowl at the ball of the second; the fourth at the ball of the third, and so on. That same order must be preserved throughout, except when the ball aimed at is 'pocketed,' or driven through one of the six openings round the court. When that happens, the player who has pocketed the ball is allowed another shot, and this time aims at the ball nearest to him, continuing to do this for the remainder of the game – which comes when all the balls but one are pocketed.

The aim of the game is to pocket balls, whilst avoiding being pocketed oneself – thus the player whose ball remains at the end has won the game.

An alternative plan is to allow each player three 'lives,' as in *pool* played on a billiard table. A player who is pocketed then loses one life; but is allowed to take his ball again when his turn comes round and bowl afresh from the end of the court. When a player has lost all three lives he is out of the game, and the winner is the one who stays in longest.

64 MINIATURE GOLF

Outfits for this interesting game are readily obtainable. Golf putters and golf balls are used, and a number of obstacles are placed about the lawn, through which players have to take their balls. If you care to make your own obstacles it is a fairly simple matter – for instance, a short tunnel, a bridge, a gateway, and perhaps some hoops like croquet hoops but much smaller. The layout of the course will depend on the ground available.

Players can play individually, or with two or more a side. Each plays with the same ball throughout. The best games result from foursomes – two a side – and other players can take part by forming other sets of four and following the first group round at a suitable distance.

The object of the game is that the player shall get round the course before his opponents, or, alternatively, shall win more obstacles than the opponent – that player 'wins' an obstacle who first gets his ball past it.

Whichever method is adopted, no player can take more than one stroke at a time, and then only in his proper turn.

It is permissible to drive a ball into the ball of an opponent, thus displacing it.

65 NET BALL

Generally seven a side take part in this, and the pitch is 100 ft. by 50 ft. For garden purposes the game can be considered the same as *basket ball*, and adaptations in measurements and playing rules can be made from both these games to suit your own purpose. It will be useful to give an outline.

The proper 'field' is divided by transverse lines into three equal sections. A circle of 2 ft. radius must be marked in the centre of the playing area. The goals are set up in the middle of each rear line, and from each post a semicircle of 16 ft. radius,

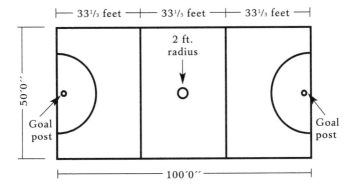

called the 'shooting circle,' is marked. The diagram shows all this.

Each goal consists of a wooden post supporting, 10 ft. from the ground, a net or basket, with no bottom. When the football which is used is tossed so that it drops through this a goal is scored.

The game is started by the referee bouncing the ball in the centre circle. After play has begun the ball may be caught or held in any way, or be thrown or struck in any direction. But no player must attempt to take the ball from another by pulling or snatching – no opponent in possession of the ball can be interfered with.

Each player must intercept the ball only when it has left the opponent's hand. When two grip the ball together, it is bounced between them by the referee.

A goal is scored when the ball is thrown or struck into the net or basket from the shooting circle or any point within it, and 2 points are counted.

The game usually consists of two halves of 15 minutes each, with a rest of not more than 5 minutes between.

In the diagram the full markings are given; actually for the friendly little garden game the two lines across do not matter – they have their significance only if you wish to play the standard game, with the official code of rules.

66 NINEPINS CROQUET

This is a combination of ninepins, or skittles, and croquet. An ordinary set of ninepins is used, the pins being stood up in the middle of the lawn, but spread rather more widely from each other than usual – a distance of 2 ft. between is very suitable.

Then the players, each with croquet or skittle balls, and mallets, play up from the end of the lawn. Each takes one stroke in turn, the object of each being to knock over as many of the pins as possible. A point is scored for each pin knocked down. When all are down the players take their balls back to the starting line;

the pins are replaced, and a new round begins.

That player wins who first scores 50 points.

Skittles knocked over should be allowed to lie until the end of the game; unless by mutual agreement every one is removed before the next stroke is made. No player can take more than one stroke at a time. If a player knocks down a pin with a mallet the pin is replaced and the player forfeits a stroke.

67 OBSTACLE CROQUET

Here is a game which is a close relation of *miniature golf*, No. 64.

Ordinary croquet balls and mallets are used, but no hoops – unless they be employed to form 'obstacles,' a number of them, for instance, making a tunnel.

Obstacles can be devised with a little ingenuity. A tunnel a couple of feet long is useful – every ball failing to pass completely through at one stroke having to be taken back to one mallet's length from the previous obstacle. Then you can have a bridge – made of a steep upward-sloping board, with a drop down on the farther side, both edges being shielded by 'walls.' Skittles may be placed at another point; it being ruled that a ball is not allowed through unless it passes without upsetting the skittles. A few sticks placed at intervals in a straight line makes another good obstacle – the ball must zigzag in and out of this line. It may be possible at another point for the ball to have to jump clean over some sort of ditch or hole, or pass round a 'bunker.'

As with miniature golf, either the winner may be the person who makes the complete round in fewest strokes, or each obstacle can be played for separately – like holes in a round of golf.

68 PIN BALL

A fairly big 'field' is needed for this. Two teams are chosen, with four to ten players in each, and any large ball like a football is used. At each end of the playing course a skittle, bottle, or

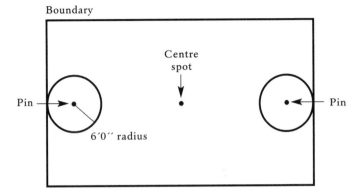

Boundary

Centre spot

Pin

Pin

6'0" radius

something similar is stood – this is the 'pin.' Round this a circle of 6 ft. radius is marked. The only other marking needed is the centre point.

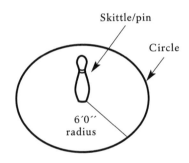

Skittle/pin

Circle

6'0" radius

The game begins at the centre, by the referee, or one of the team leaders, tossing up the ball – and then play starts.

The aim of each team is to knock over the pin of their opponents, and whenever this is achieved a goal is scored, and the game is restarted.

No kicking of the ball is allowed at any point of the game. The ball must be caught and thrown. Neither is it permitted for a player to carry the ball. He must throw it from the point where he caught it – unless he takes it along by bouncing it on the ground. Tackling, in the football sense, is also ruled out, though it is permissible to grab at a ball which another player is holding or bouncing.

Thus the game consists chiefly of rapid passing, and combination work. And, as rough play cannot well come in, the game is quite suitable for mixed teams.

In scoring goals the ball must always be thrown from some point outside the circle marked round the pin. No player, either defender or attacker, must step inside this circle.

There is little need to have a team apportioned out as goalkeeper, backs, and so on; the best plan is to let the trend of the game determine what strategy is desirable, and what placings. But, of course, there is no reason why you should not have someone always standing to protect the pin, if you wish.

Whenever the ball goes outside the field of play it should be brought to the boundary at the point where it passed out, and thrown in by a player – the nearest one – of the opposite team to that which was responsible for it going out. The same rule applies at the end of the 'field'; there are no such things as the 'goal kicks' of football.

69 PUTTING

The making of a golf hole has been described in the last chapter of the book.

Clock golf and *spiral golf*, Nos. 56 and 46, are really both of them plain putting games; but they have the paraphernalia of numbers and fixed shapes and starting points to give novelty and added interest to the players.

The keen golfer, however, needs no such adjunct, and given a lawn of sufficient quality can be perfectly happy with straightforward putting to a hole in the centre.

Get variety of approach by playing from all points of the compass, and imitate actual golfing conditions as nearly as possible in all particulars. Having got your turf in sound condition be careful not to let other games upset it. If, as is natural, you do want to enjoy some of the other suggestions of this book, it may be practicable to preserve a narrow strip up one side or across one end of your lawn for your putting.

70 ROBBER CROQUET

Any number of players can take part in this, providing each has his or her own ball. Ordinary croquet equipment is used, and the hoops are arranged in the usual way, or in any more convenient fashion.

Each player takes one stroke in turn – the first strokes of the game must be from a starting line; after that players may go to any hoops they choose, in any order. When a ball goes through a hoop one more stroke is allowed. A point is scored for every hoop which is thus passed.

At any time, however, a player may drive his ball at any other ball, and if he makes a hit he robs the ball's owner of any score he may happen to have, the number of points taken being not more than ten. The points thus taken are added to the score of the robber.

When a player reaches ten points they are safely 'banked,' and cannot be taken from him. But, of course, any points beyond that are liable to be stolen, until their total again reaches ten, when they too are banked.

The points to be reached by the winner – 40, 50, 60 – should be agreed on beforehand.

There is plenty of fun in this game, and excitement, as well as real opportunity for sound croquet play and tactical skill.

71 TAG BALL

Almost any number can take part in this very interesting variant of *tag*. The fact that a ball is used restricts the movement of players sufficiently to make the game possible on quite small lawns. But there is plenty of strenuous fun.

A fairly large ball, or football, is used, and this must not be kicked, but propelled about by hand. It must not be picked up or thrown, but simply pushed along the ground.

One player is *It*, and his aim is to overtake and touch the ball; until he succeeds in doing this he must remain *It*. But when he is successful, that player who last touched the ball becomes *It*, and must in turn pursue the ball to gain release.

The object of the other players is to keep the ball moving so that *It* is unable to overtake it. They must play the ball whenever it comes in their direction – even at the risk of becoming *It*.

Players should not obstruct or hamper *It* in any way, their sole method of opposing him must be by keeping the ball moving all the time, out of his reach.

72 TARGET BALL

This is another game in which almost any number can take part.

Two teams are chosen, and each has an innings, which must be timed, for it is the team whose innings lasts longest which wins.

One or more small soft balls are needed – their number will depend on the number of players.

The team which is to have its first innings stands in the middle of the lawn, spread apart as widely as circumstances will permit; while the other team stands round, enclosing them in a large circle. The team forming the circle should keep back at a reasonable distance – it may be an advantage to have a ring marked on the ground inside which they may not go.

Then the game begins. Those standing round have the balls, and start to throw them at the players in the middle. Every player struck by a ball drops out of the ring – and the throwing continues until all the inner team have been hit, and their innings is completed. Of course the players in the middle can dodge as they like. But they must not touch or pick up the balls – to touch a ball with the hand is as fatal as being hit by it.

When it happens that a ball stays in the ring one of the throwing team may dash in and recover it; but he must not take a throw with it until he has returned to his proper place outside the ring. Any member of the 'out' team may throw. There is no order in the throwing; whenever a ball comes to him the player simply picks it up and takes a throw.

After one innings is over the teams change places, and the new team begins to throw.

73 TOSS BALL

There is no better garden game than this for any number of players up to a dozen.

A net about 6 ft. high is required, and court markings as described in the last chapter of this book; the general manner of play should also be according to the Net Game Rules in *Chapter 5*.

Either a net ball or football can be used, or a large rubber bladder, preferably strengthened with strips of rubber or canvas, in the common manner of children's playballs.

The opposing teams of two to six a side stand in their respective halves on either side of the net, and the game begins by one player serving across from a base line into the diagonally opposite court. A round-arm fling is used and the ball is necessarily thrown in an upward direction, to clear the net. Always it must be thrown upwards. The opposing side catch and return the ball – if they can.

Every time the ball touches the ground a point is lost – if the ball touches in the court it is the receiver who forfeits the point; if the ball comes to ground outside the court, then the point is forfeited by the side which made the throw – unless of course a player allows the ball to fall outside after it has touched or bounced against him, for then he is responsible.

The ball must not be held or carried; it should be tossed immediately it is caught. It is not necessary that it should be tossed back across the net; it may pass through the hands of two or more people on the same side of the net, and often good strategic work can be done by a quick pass before the ball is returned.

One or both hands can be used for catching and tossing. The ball must always be fairly caught before being returned; it should not be punched or volleyed in any way – any such act, like a kick, forfeits a point to the offender.

When toss ball is played with singles or doubles the proper observance of half courts and the automatic procedure for serving and receiving is straightforward enough, according to the Net Game Rules. When, however, more than four are taking part each team should arrange its order of players for serving and receiving services, and the half courts can be observed or ignored just as best suits circumstances. Often, with a fairly large number, anyone of a team can be allowed to receive a service. With big numbers, too, it is advisable that a team leader shall appoint where his players shall take up their positions, otherwise they may hamper each other.

74 TREASURE HUNT

This is not a strenuous, and hardly a competitive game, but it can give plenty of harmless fun at a friendly little garden party, and it can make a pleasing relaxation from the more ordinary items of garden games programme.

First, mark out a section of your lawn, several yards square, in which the treasure hunt is to take place. Then look this piece of ground over carefully, and decide just where you really would, if you had need, bury your 'treasure' – which may be a box of chocolates, or anything of the sort. Use genuine judgment, trying to spot the place where you could expect to make your hiding-place with least trouble and disturbance of the ground. Then, having decided, take a piece of paper and draw a small-scale plan of the patch of lawn, marking on it the precise place where you have decided the treasure should be hidden. Of course, you will give none of your players any inkling of your reasonings and decision, and you will keep the paper out of their sight.

The treasure hunters then begin. Each in turn makes his

examination of the patch of ground, and arrives at his own conclusions as to the most likely spot for the concealment of the treasure. Having found this spot, each sticks a small flag or stick or label, fastened to a pin, in the ground – the name of the person may be written on the label.

When all have done their best you will bring out your key plan and reveal the actual spot chosen by you. This can then be shown on the patch of turf – and the player whose flag or pin is nearest the original spot wins the treasure.

75 VOLLEY BALL

This excellent and fast game is very much like *toss ball* No. 73, and like that is governed by the same court markings and Net Game Rules of *Chapter 5*. A net similarly 6 ft. high is also used.

But instead of being caught and tossed the ball must always be volleyed. It is a fault for a player to hold it either in one or both hands, and a point is thereby forfeited. The game consequently is very fast, and it may be advisable to have the court rather smaller than the usual 40 ft. by 18 ft. unless you have a fair number of players.

To begin the game one person serves from the back corner of the court. He tosses the ball into the air from his left hand, and, as it is falling, punches it hard with his right – driving it across the net in the ordinary manner. Should he fail to make a good serve, he is, of course, entitled to another.

The player receiving the ball must immediately volley it, either by punching with the fist or striking with flat palms. Both hands may be used together in a sort of vigorous push, providing that they do not in any way hold the ball.

As in *toss ball*, it is not essential that a player shall immediately return the ball over the net. He may instead pass to another player of his own side. Often, when the ball is received right at the back of the court it is impossible to do more than keep it in the air, and gradually work it back from player to player towards the net, where someone is in a good position to make an effective return.

Should a player drop the ball or fail to return it over the net so that it falls to the ground, he forfeits a point for his side. It is not a fault for a player to keep the ball in the air when it is actually outside the court; but if an opponent has driven it across the net in such a fashion that it is likely to fall outside the court the best plan for the receiving side is to let it fall, and so secure the point.

Any large, sufficiently strong ball will serve for this game. A small football is ideal, providing the lace is so secured that it cannot hurt knuckles.

CHAPTER FOUR

GAMES FOR
THE CHILDREN

76 BADTEN

This is a sort of simple mixture of badminton and tennis. Two can play, but it is better fun to have four. A net 5 ft. high is needed, and it is good to have at least the outside line of the court markings as they are described in the last chapter of this book.

Padders also are required – how to make these is also told in the same *Chapter 5*. Or, of course, you may buy padders from a sports dealer – padders are simply solid wood rackets.

The only other thing you need is a badminton shuttle, and the heavy outdoor kind is best.

The game starts by one player serving the shuttle over the net, to the player in the diagonally opposite court, and that one returns the shuttle to the player opposite to him – not diagonally opposite. Then this third player returns again to the fourth player, who is diagonally opposite and has not yet had a stroke. And finally this last player hits the shuttle straight across the net to the player who began the game.

The diagram (right) shows this.

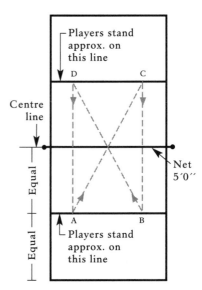

Thus each player in turn receives and passes the shuttle back across the net – if he can.

There is no attempt to place the shuttle so that the other player cannot play it; in fact, your chief concern is just the opposite – you hope that he will play it, for unless he does your chance of future scores is lost. In this respect the game differs from all ordinary net games.

Note: Dotted lines show direction of 'shots'

The scoring is as follows:

The first player to strike the shuttle scores 1 point; the second, if he safely receives and makes his hit, counts 2; the third, receiving and hitting in his turn, counts 3 – and so on. In this way the scoring piles up, and only stops when one player fails to follow on. Supposing the last player to make his stroke counted 13 and the next fails to hit the shuttle, then all four players would reckon as their scores the last numbers that they counted. Play would then begin again.

It is helpful to have a scorer with pencil and paper because there are usually rather awkward reckonings to be made. It may be agreed on beforehand that the first player to reach 50 points has won the game.

There is one thing that may spoil the game – players getting too close to the net, so that instead of taking really long shots they just pat the shuttle backwards and forwards a yard or two. To prevent this it is helpful if marks be put on the ground, half-way up each court, so that players are compelled to keep behind these.

77 BAT, TRAP AND BALL

The bat, trap and ball can easily be bought – for this is one of the oldest and most popular of children's games.

Any number of players can take part; eight or ten is the best number. These are divided into two teams, and each in turn takes an innings, as in cricket.

The 'in' side sends in one member at a time, while the fielding side stand round at a suitable distance. The player with the bat places the ball on the trap, then strikes the trigger with the bat and so shoots the ball into the air. Before it can fall he drives it any direction he chooses. If a fielder catches it before it reaches the ground, not only the batsman but the whole of his team are put out. But if it reaches the ground the fielder who first picks it up stands at the point where he recovered it and takes a throw at the trap. Should the ball hit the trap the batsman is put out; should the ball miss, the batsman counts one point.

The batsman, of course, continues batting until he is put out. It should be arranged beforehand whether the trap is to be placed broadside on to any fielder making a throw – generally this is done.

Scores are reckoned as an innings proceeds, and the team which makes the biggest total wins.

Just two players can have plenty of enjoyment, though it will be harder for the fielder – unless he is allowed always to throw from a fixed point.

78 BELL AND HOOP

If there is a tree on your lawn, or anywhere else in the garden, this game can be enjoyed.

From a branch suspend a small hoop, and in the middle of the hoop hang a bell – or something that will sound when it is hit, like a piece of metal tubing, a horseshoe, a tin, flat piece of iron.

Then the players stand at a suitable distance, perhaps five yards, where a throwing line is marked, and begin to toss balls at the hoop.

For every ball that rings the bell, 5 points are counted; for a ball that goes through the hoop without ringing the bell, 3 points; for a ball that hits the hoop but does not go through, 1 point. The first player to reach 50 points wins the game.

If teams are taking part the members of each team should toss alternately, and there should be someone who will write down everybody's scores.

Instead of balls, beanbags may be used. These can be easily procured from any sports dealer, or made in the manner described in the last chapter of this book.

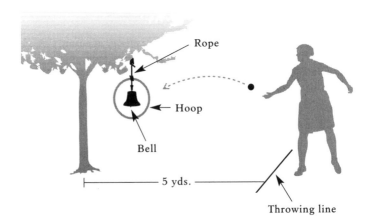

79 BLOWPIPE TARGET

Plenty of fun can be had from a blowpipe – as used by the Indians of South America. Any boy can make his own equipment.

First the blowpipe itself. This should be 4 or 5 ft. long. A length of light metal curtain rod can be used, but it will be necessary to glue a band of brown paper round it, spiral fashion, to cover the joint up its side and so make it airtight. As the blowpipe itself should be only about half an inch in diameter, it is necessary also to have a mouthpiece at the end of larger size. The easiest plan is to get a small tin funnel, just large enough to let the lips press into it. The spout of this funnel can then be slit up until it will slide down over the end of the tube, and it can then be bound firmly into position by close-wrapped string.

Another, and better, way of making a blowpipe is to use only paper, stiffened with shellac and glue. But this is more trouble.

Get an iron rod or stick of half-inch diameter – it must be perfectly straight – and coat it with wax so that your paper will not stick. Then use 9-in. strips of brown paper, winding them on spiral fashion, so that each strip overlaps half the previous coil. Where one strip finishes glue on the next, so that there are no loose edges left inside. After covering your full length, coat the whole

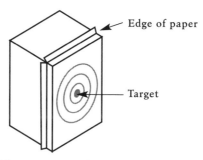

Edge of paper

Target

The entire target hole is cut out of lid, then paper with target painted on is shut in and held taut by lid

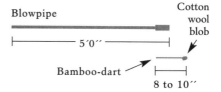

Blowpipe

Cotton wool blob

5′0″

Bamboo-dart

8 to 10″

with shellac, pretty thickly. As soon as this has dried sufficiently to be sticky, wrap round a second layer of paper just as you did the first, keeping it straight and smooth, though you may make your spiral in the opposite direction, for added strength. Coat again with shellac – and continue until you have put on six layers of paper in the same fashion. When the whole thing is dry and stiff, slip out the rod and carefully trim the ends. You will then have a hard clean tube, as strong almost as one of metal.

Finally fix a mouthpiece. This is a 4-in. length of tube made similarly, but round a piece of broom-handle or something of the sort. When this is finished it should slip on and be glued tightly to the blowpipe – at the end which allows the dart to pass down the tube without catching the edges of the paper.

Smear some oil down inside the length of tubing, and give the outside a coat of shellac – and it will be ready for use.

The dart is easily made. A thin splinter of bamboo cane, less than half as thick as a pencil, and 8 to 10 in. long. Scrape and glasspaper it until it is round and perfectly straight. Put a blunt point to it, and to the other end bind with cotton, or fix with a spot of glue, a blob of cotton wool about as big as a thimble. Then you are ready, all but the target. This can be a piece of paper from a writing-pad, with circles drawn or painted on it, or any larger piece of moderately soft paper. Get a cardboard box – a boot-box will serve, and cut a large circular hole in the lid. All you have to do then is to put your paper target inside the lid and shut the lid down on to the box, thus holding the paper taut and secure. The marked target, of course, shows through the hole in the lid.

Stand the target 5 to 10 yds. away and take up your blowpipe. Insert a dart, point first, and push down the woolly end a couple of inches along the tube. Grip the blowpipe firmly with both hands and press the mouthpiece over your lips. A sharp puff will then send the dart straight and hard at the target.

With practice you may send the dart surprising distances.

80 BOLAS SWINGING

Cowboys in South America use the bolas – or lasso with two balls at the end – for entangling the legs of cattle and so bringing them down and capturing them. Your own bolas work will consist only of capturing a cardboard box or something of that sort – but there will be plenty of enjoyment in it.

A strong, upple, light cord, not quite so thick as a clothes line, is needed. It should be 5 or 6 yds. long. Take another piece a yard long and tie one end of it to the other cord at a point 3 ft. from the end. Thus you will have a long cord with a double end, as shown in the diagram.

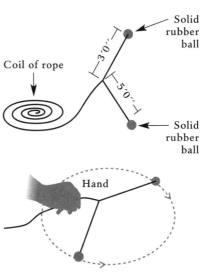

To the end of each of these short tongues a rubber ball must be attached. The best method is to get a small solid or sponge rubber ball; pierce it and thread the cord through, then knot the cord end on the farther side. The bolas is now complete.

Before attempting to throw the bolas you must get the knack of setting the balls swinging. While the bolas is travelling through the air the balls are revolving rapidly in circles around each other, and when they reach their target they immediately wrap round it. So that before they are thrown they must be revolving.

If you grip the rope with one hand at the point where it divides into two it will be an easy matter to set both balls circling in a 5- to 6-ft. circle. But that is not what is required – the balls must not circle in the *same*, but in *opposite* directions. The diagram shows this. Some patience is required to get the knack of this double circling, but once it is acquired the thing is easy.

Place the two balls on the ground, as far from each other as possible. Then grip the main cord just where the two ends join. If you now jerk your hand up until it is about at shoulder-level in front of you, the balls will naturally drop down and close towards each other as they clear the ground. Thus at this moment they are actually travelling towards each other – in *opposite directions*. And if they have sufficient momentum they will continue to travel in their same directions even when they have met, so that they will pass each other and go on round in circles – just as the diagram indicates. To keep them circling in this fashion it is necessary only to move your hand sharply up and down a few inches, thus adding regularly to the impetus of each.

All the preceding may sound rather complicated, but once you try it out with an actual bolas it will become clear.

Persevere until you can keep the balls circling, passing and repassing each other, above your head, at a really good pace – using the same short backward and forward wrist movement to keep them going. And then you will be ready to try a throw. Add a full arm sweep to the wrist action, and let your bolas fly, like a lasso, at your object – the cardboard box or chair. The right hand will make the throw; the left will guide the slack of the cord until it flies clear.

With a good throw the balls, of course, will be circling all the time during their flight, so that when they reach the target they will coil round from opposite directions, enclosing it tightly. You then dash upon the scene; seize the end of the main cord – and there you have your 'captive' under control!

But don't try to capture *people*!

81 BOOMERANG THROWING

Boomerangs can be bought quite cheaply, or you can make your own.

To make one get a piece of ash 2 ft. long, 5 in. wide, and $3/8$ in. thick. Cut from this two pieces, shaped as in the diagram – the longer piece is 18 in. from end to end. The tapering is from $1^3/4$ in. at the narrowest point to $2^1/4$ in. at the widest part, where the curve is. Fasten these two pieces together, by a halving joint, with glue and small screws, so that the whole is like one solid piece of wood. Now you must taper down the edges of your boomerang, leaving the centre at the original thickness, but cutting away so that from the centre the wood slopes away on either side down to an edge thickness of about $1/8$ in. When you have smoothed and rounded and streamlined the whole thing the boomerang is finished – though you may improve the appearance by rubbing with linseed oil. But be very careful that every bit of the wood is smooth and rounded – there must be neither roughness nor sharp edges if the boomerang is to fly well.

Now for making a throw.

Grip one end of the boomerang in your right hand, with the points kept forward, and stretch your arm back behind your

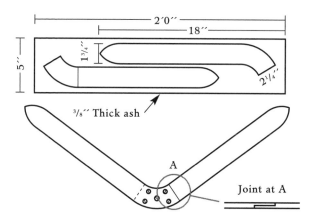

shoulder. Fling forward the straight arm with quick vigour, and a sort of rounded overarm swing, and, when the boomerang is right at the front, give it a smart flick as if you were cracking a whiplash. At the same instant release it smoothly.

The boomerang will sail forward, for perhaps 20 or 30 yds., and then will swerve sideways and upwards, and come whirling back towards you, its direction changed as the spin of the wood overcomes the forward impetus of the throw.

But – you must throw into the wind if the boomerang is to come back. The trick can't be done otherwise.

82 BOTTLE FISHING

Stand up a row of bottles a foot or so apart, then supply each player with a 'fishing rod,' and see who can catch his bottle first.

All that you need for the fishing rod is a stick or cane 3 to 5 ft. long, with a string of the same length tied to the end. At the tip of the string is fastened a brass ring – large enough to go over the neck of a bottle.

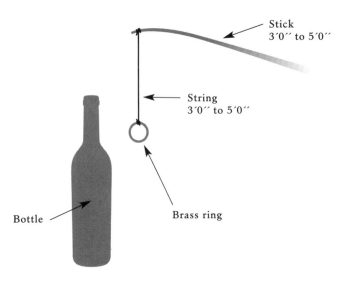

Stick
3´0˝ to 5´0˝

String
3´0˝ to 5´0˝

Bottle

Brass ring

Until you have tried to get a bottle neck in this fashion you cannot realize what a troublesome job it is, for of course the ring hangs vertically, not horizontally, from the string.

Count one point for a player when he catches his bottle – the test is pulling the bottle over just as if a fish were being landed. The first player to score 10 points wins the game. After each 'catch' the bottle is replaced, and all players start afresh.

83 BUCKET TAG

A 'home line' is marked at one end of the lawn. Near the other end stands the player who is *It*, with his back to the home line. And in front of him, about 3 yds. farther on, is a bucket. On the right-hand side of *It*, a yard or two away, is a cluster of players; and on the left-hand side another similar cluster. They all watch him anxiously.

It has a ball. He tries to toss it into the bucket. If it does not go in nothing happens – except that he has to fetch the ball back for another try. But when he does succeed in getting the ball into the bucket, that is the signal for all the other players to make a dash for the home line – and *It* runs after them. Anyone he manages to tag before the line is reached changes places with *It*, and the game goes on as before.

It need not recover the ball from the bucket before setting in pursuit of the rest; he, like them, is free to run the instant the ball is safely in the bucket. The runners have only a slight advantage over him – they are facing the home line at the moment of starting, while he is facing the bucket and has to turn round before he can follow them.

Players must not be allowed to stand too far out from *It* while they are waiting for his throws.

If no bucket is handy the game can be played just as well with a small hole in the ground, towards which the ball can be rolled.

84 A CHUTE

You can, if you prefer, buy your equipment ready-made.

To make a chute or slide for children is a job for a carpenter, or an amateur woodworker of considerable experience. The thing must be strong; it must be rigid, and it must be so smoothed that there is no danger of splinters or sharp edges.

Some hard wood like elm is desirable, and, though much more trouble and expense are involved, the chute is much improved if it can be lined with brass or some rust-proof metal. But there can be plenty of fun from a plain wood chute, down which youngsters can glide on a mat, or in sturdy clothes.

The simplest sort of chute is a plain, straight trough with shallow, flatly sloping sides. It could be 10 ft. long, and fall from a height of 6 ft. down to 1 ft. The greatest care needs to be taken to

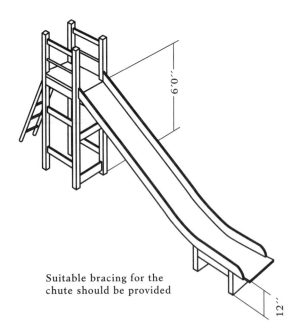

Suitable bracing for the
chute should be provided

make its top end rigid. A ladder can be fixed behind the head, and a rail be put on either side where the youngster gets on. See that every part of the chute which can possibly be touched or clutched is smooth.

If the chute is lined with metal so that the slider is likely to come down at a pretty fast pace it is advisable to flatten out the end so that speed can slacken before the slider gets off.

With a higher, more ambitious chute, several turns can be included, but don't have these too sharp, and be particularly careful that each corner is solid and smooth. Such a chute as this, of course, needs to have high sides, so that the slider is safely enclosed.

It is worth-while considering the ground at the foot of the chute. Don't let it be your choicest bit of turf, for rough feet will soon stamp the grass out of existence.

85 CUBBYHOLE

A cubbyhole is an ideal thing for youngsters of two to six. It should be built in a sunny corner of the garden, preferably against the back of garage or shed – providing there is no danger that the children will later use it as a stepping-stone to the roof!

The essential features of a cubbyhole are the body part, which may be a large box roomy enough for two or three children to sit in; a sloping plank leading from the ground into this box, and up which the children can crawl; a short ladder, forming an alternative means of entry or egress.

Your large wooden box should be fixed perhaps 3 ft. from the ground, lying on its side, with its open top facing outwards – thus it forms an open-fronted 'room' in which the kiddies can sit, with their feet drawn up inside or dangling over the front edge. The 'roof,' which will be one of the original sides of the box, can be raised at one end and covered with felt to make it weatherproof and allow wet to run off.

One end should be knocked from the box, and at this open

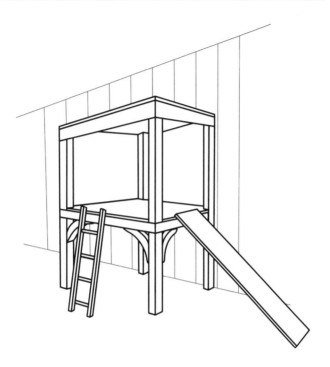

end the plank can arrive. The plank should be fairly wide, and very smooth. Unless it is of hard wood it should be treated with some preservative that will not rub off, or with paint. But, if it is painted, you had better make sure from the outset that the youngsters understand they should not slide down the plank, for a rough surface can play havoc with clothes!

The ladder should not protrude above the edge of the box, and should be fixed at the end opposite to the plank, it will arrive at the front edge.

See that all edges are smooth and rounded, so that there is no danger from nails or splinters, and have the whole strong enough to withstand the pretty hard usage it will inevitably get.

Your grocer will doubtless be able to supply the big sturdy box with which you can start your structure.

86 FOUR-WAY BALL

For this simple little game all that is required is a chair and a ball. Any number of players can take part.

Place the chair in the middle of the lawn, or any clear, hard bit of garden, and let the players stand round.

Each player in turn rolls the ball towards the chair four times, once from each side – north, east, south, west – and from a distance of about 4 yds. If he gets the ball clean under from the north he counts 1 point; if with the next throw he gets the ball under from the east, he counts an additional 2 points; if he scores again from the south, 3 points are added; and if his fourth throw is also successful, from the west, then he is allowed 4 points more – making his total 10 points.

If, however, he fails at any throw, the next player takes the ball and begins his throws in the same manner. Every player in turn does what he can; then the whole round begins afresh.

The first player to score 50 points, or any other agreed number, wins the game.

It is advisable to have a bowling line clearly marked on each side of the chair so that all players stand at the same distance.

87 GIANT PUSHBALL

Not everyone has a big pushball, of course. But if you have there will be plenty of scope for enjoyment on the lawn.

With just one or two players the best games consist of vaulting, jumping, and so on – trying to vault right on to the ball, for instance, so that the boy or girl can stand upright on it, and remain whilst counting ten.

Then there can be contests, with court markings, and one or more players on each side. That side scores a point which pushes the ball over the opponents' rear line. Five points can be *game*.

With a larger number of players, say a dozen, get them to lie down in a circle, on their backs, with their feet towards the centre. The players number round – the *evens* becoming one team and the *odds* the other. The ball is put on the ground at the centre, and then the tussle begins. Only the feet are allowed to touch the ball, and players must remain flat on their backs throughout. The evens try for five minutes to kick the ball out of the ring, over the players' heads: the odds do their best to keep it in. A point is counted each time the evens succeed in getting the ball out, and a restart is made. At the end of five minutes the teams take a change – the odds trying to get the ball out and the evens to keep it in. The game is won by the team which, after the full ten minutes, has scored most points.

A still better game with two teams of about the same size is to have the sides in two straight rows, lying similarly on their backs, feet inwards. There is thus an avenue down between the two rows of feet, when the players are at rest. The ball is then rolled into the middle – and each team strives to drive it clean over its opponents. No handling is, of course, allowed. A point is counted each time the ball rolls behind the heads of either team.

88 JAVELIN FLING

First make your javelin. A slim straight piece of stick 12 to 20 in. long is needed. Make a blunt point at one end, and weight it, by binding it with wire, driving in a heavy nail, or fastening some piece of metal to it – actually it hardly matters whether the javelin has a point. Then at the rear end of the stick, make a slit and wedge into it a feather, or piece of tin or stiff paper; insert a similar piece crossways – so that you have three, or four, 'blades,' and your javelin is 'feathered' in the manner of an arrow. The javelin is really like an arrow with a weighted point.

Now for the target. First a square piece of board, about 12 in. across. On this nail or screw a tin – a toffee tin measuring about 9 in. across, and circular, will do. The bottom of the tin is

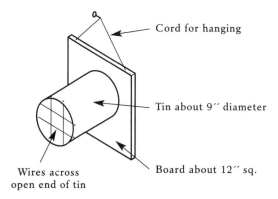

Cord for hanging

Tin about 9″ diameter

Board about 12″ sq.

Wires across
open end of tin

secured to the board, and the lid is not required. This board can be hung from the branch of a tree, like a dart board, the tin will then face towards the marksman. But the tin is not yet finished. Eight holes will have been punched in its edges, and through these four pieces of wire will have been threaded – as shown in the diagram. The ends of the wire can be bent over so that they do not slip out.

These wires, it will be seen, divide the front, open end of the tin into nine sections. The purpose of them is to ensure that the dart remains in whichever part of the 'target' it enters, so that scoring can be determined.

Players stand at a throwing line about 5 yds. from the suspended target, and each takes one turn to throw the javelin.

When the javelin enters the centre square of the target it scores 5 points; when it goes into any of the other sections 3 points are counted; when it hits the board 1 point is reckoned. That player wins the game who first scores 50.

89 JUNGLE CLIMB

This is a delightful thing for boys or girls of from four to ten. But it can hardly be made except by a skilled workman, though it can be bought ready-made. It consists of a jumble of bars,

firmly fixed, among
which youngsters can
climb. Every bar must
be thoroughly secure.
Wood can be used
for the structure,
but galvanized iron
piping is better. Such
a structure can
have properly fitted
junction and angle
pieces, and be
made into such an
elaborate thing that
the imaginative child
can readily conceive

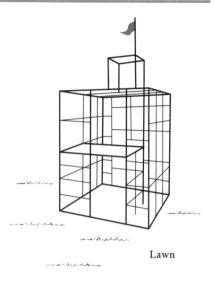

Lawn

himself a sort of Tarzan clambering through forest boughs.

There is, of course, real exercise and athletic value in a
good jungle climb.

Youngsters, on this basic structure, can build up all sorts of
things – houses, ships, airplanes, and so on. The diagram gives
some idea of possible form.

90 LARIAT THROWING

A cotton cord of ³/₈-in. diameter is needed for this. It should be
plaited not twisted cord, and the best length is about 30 ft. Of
course you may buy your lariat ready-made. To make one all that
is necessary is to put a 3-in. loop at one end through which the
other end can be threaded. This loop is called the 'honda.'

Coil the rope into the left hand and with the right hand
hold a big loop of it, gripping both 'stem,' or main part of the
cord, and the big loop itself about 18 in. above the honda – this is
shown in the diagram. The honda must be on the outer side of
your right hand.

Now take your stand about 3 or 4 yds. from a chair or post, and prepare to make your first throw.

Keeping your right arm straight, raise it above your head, and swing it round, or rather flick the wrist round, in a small circle, in the direction opposite to that in which the hands of a clock travel. If you do this properly – probably you won't at first – you will find the big loop of cord circling flatly over your head, keeping well spread and open. When you have whirled it round several times, and have it well open, then hurl it forward, stepping forward towards your target at the same time. The loop should fly through the air and, if it is accurately aimed, will settle over the chair or post. The coiled cord, of course, will slip freely from your left hand, in which the fingers are merely hooked to form a sort of peg. Finally, when your loop has caught the object you can haul the lariat tight, because the end of it will still be retained between thumb and first finger of your left hand.

A lot of practice is needed to become expert with the lariat. But persevere, and soon you will be able to stand farther back – 20 and even 30 ft.

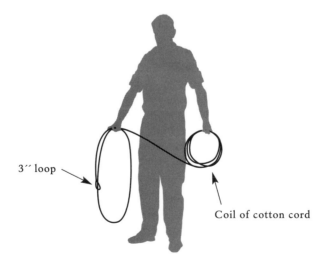

3˝ loop

Coil of cotton cord

91 PUNCTURE SPOT

An old motor tyre is needed for this game. Put it down flat in the middle of the lawn, and get all the boys and girls who are to take part to stand around in a circle, facing inwards and clasping hands.

Then they begin moving round, each trying to pull or push his or her neighbour on to the tyre. Anyone stepping on the tyre is said to have 'punctured' it, and so drops out of the game.

Continue until all have fallen out but the last – who is thus the winner.

There is plenty of hard exertion in this game, and plenty of agile leaping, backwards and forwards, is necessary.

Warn all your players against loosing their handclasps, in order to avoid being dragged on to the tyre.

92 ROPE SPINNING

If you have been interested in *lariat throwing* (No. 90), then rope spinning will naturally follow on. You will use the same plaited, not twisted, cotton cord, of $^3/_8$-in, diameter, but now it need only be about 3 or 4 yds. long. The same loop or 'honda' is needed, through which the free end can be threaded. In fact, the preliminary circling over the head with which you begin a lariat throw is really a simple form of rope spinning.

But the flat or horizontal loop is the first thing to learn. Hold the big loop as shown in the first part of the diagram.

Only one finger is keeping up the loop, in the right hand; the others are gripping the end of the cord. The left hand lightly holds the big loop farther along. Now, with a quick outward flick of the right hand, and a releasing of the left, set the loop flatly circling as shown in the second part of the diagram. Once you get this flat, spinning movement, it is fairly easy to keep it going by a strong circular twisting of the wrist. You may enlarge the circle by letting more of the stem slip down through the honda.

A lot of practice is needed to get this flat spin strong and even, but when you have mastered it you can go on with confidence.

Try next jumping inside your loop, and making it circle round you, by changing the cord end from hand to hand. You can lift the loop up the body until it is spinning round the head.

Afterwards try reverse spins; and vertical spins in front of and behind the body. Always it is the same principle. The hand is a sort of wheel hub, and the stem of the cord down to the honda a sort of spoke, and the hub must keep the spoke going round, carrying with it the rim of the wheel – which is the loop.

It is advisable to let the end of the cord revolve freely in your hand, otherwise the cord will become twisted and kinks will spoil the spinning.

93 SEESAW

It is not difficult to construct a seesaw in the garden. If it is to stay there the whole year round the plank should be painted, like the frame, and a really solid structure can be fitted by a carpenter, with an iron spindle on which the plank turns, and so on.

A much simpler structure consists of a couple of small tripods supporting a cross bar, on which the plank lies. This plank can have two cross-pieces nailed underneath it, which hold the plank in place. A simple seesaw of this description, made of two-by-three wood, can be dismantled when not in use. Length of plank and height of frames are not here given, as they must be determined by the size of the children who are to use it.

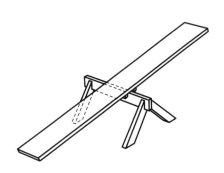

94 STILTS

All boys like stilts, and plenty of fun can be obtained from them. Of course they can be bought, like most of the other equipment in this section of the book, but they can also be made, quite easily.

Broom handles will serve for the earliest pair, for the 'steps' must not be too high. Just a foot above the ground may be sufficient for the small learner. Later, he may grow to want steps a yard above the ground, with correspondingly tall poles. Always have your poles of tough wood, like ash, which combines strength with lightness. The step should protrude about 3 in., and should be level, or tilted slightly inward so that it tends to keep the foot from slipping off.

With your first broom-handle stilts simply flatten a part of the side, the necessary height from the ground, and screw on a triangular block of hard wood for the step.

In walking on stilts the legs should be kept close against the poles, and the hands should never relax their grip. Let the stilt handles come close under the armpits, or up by the shoulders.

95 SWING

A handy garden swing of moderate size and simplicity is shown in the diagram.

posts 7′0″ high

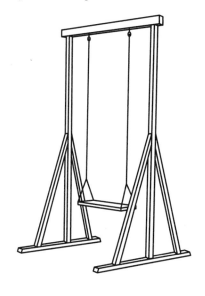

All the wood is 'four by two.' The cross-piece at the top is edgeways, not flat, and its ends are sunk in grooves at the tops of the posts. Both posts and sloping supports, which give rigidity, are dropped about a foot into the ground, and bedded tightly, with stones well rammed round them, A coating of creosote or other preservative will help the structure to stand for many years – but the cord and swing seat should be taken in during bad weather. Proper hooks and swing ropes can be readily bought at most popular stores and sports dealers.

96 TOSS TYRE

For this interesting little game beanbags are needed. They can be bought from any sports shop, or quite easily made – according to the description given in the last chapter of this book. An old motor tyre is the only other thing required.

The tyre is laid flat in the middle of the lawn, or at one end, and the players stand at equal distances round it, or at a single straight throwing line. Each in turn tosses six beanbags at the tyre, and the score is reckoned when all have been thrown, as follows:

3 points for each bag on the ground within the tyre.

2 points for each bag resting on the tyre, but touching the ground inside.

1 point for each bag resting on the tyre and not touching the ground.

The first player to score 50 points wins the game.

97 TYRE QUOITS

One or more old motor tyres are also required for this game – any garage is glad to get rid of such tyres. In addition you will need a strong upright peg at the end of the lawn. This peg should be about 12 in. high – how to make one that can be removed or fixed at will is told in *Chapter 5*.

The players stand at the bowling line 5 to 10 yds. from the peg. Each in turn bowls the tyre, and one point is scored when it falls against the peg without encircling it. When it drops clean over the peg 3 points are reckoned. The winner is he who first gets 21 points.

It is an advantage to have a peg at each end of the course, and players standing by each peg. Then the tyre does not have to be fetched back after each attempt – for it goes to each set of players in turn. Either individuals or teams can, of course, take part.

98 TYRE WRESTLING

Two old motor tyres are needed this time, and two players take part.

The tyres are laid on the ground side by side, and one player stands in each tyre. Then the two boys grip each other's shoulders and the wrestling begins.

That one wins who first compels his opponent to set foot on the ground outside his tyre.

It is possible to have three tyres, in triangle formation, and three wrestlers. First one is defeated, then the remaining two compete until the winner is settled.

99 WHIP SPORT

Plenty of fun can be had from a long-thonged whip.

To make such a whip a 3-ft. piece of broom-handle is suitable – the lower part can be bound with waxed thread to afford a better grip. For the thong have a length of pliable leather about 10 ft. long, tapering from $3/4$ in. down to $1/4$ in. If you cannot get a single piece, several bits – of an old belt for example – will serve if riveted together. Fasten the wide end of the thong into a slit at the top of your handle, with brads. Through the narrow end thread a 3-in. piece of thin cord, well frayed, almost like a tassel – this will help the 'crack' of the whip.

Now for the use of your whip. First learn to crack it, Let it trail out straight on the ground behind you, then suddenly fling your arm, gripping the handle tightly, up over the shoulder and head, and down with a quick flick in front of you. It will need a few attempts, but persevere until you get the loud crack. Then try cracking across in front of you, from side to side.

After that you can go on to hitting a target – not a live one!

Put up a couple of cricket stumps and a light piece of stick across for the bail. Aim straight, just as in a plain crack – and try to wrap the tip of your lash over the stick and so drag it off. Later you may even bring it flying back so that it can be caught in your free hand.

Another trick is to tumble small tins or skittles from a box placed on the ground at a suitable distance in front of you.

100 YO-YO

A yo-yo can be bought for a few pence, and plenty of fun can be had from it. It consists of two circular pieces of wood joined by a spindle to which a string is attached. The string should be about 2 to 3 ft. long, and a loop at the top end secures it to the middle finger.

With the string completely coiled round the spindle drop the yo-yo so that it spins rapidly as it falls. When it reaches the bottom of the string the speed of the downward fling from your hand should be sufficient to make it want to continue its revolving, so that if you give it a gentle but sharp upward pull at the correct instant it will begin to travel upwards, climbing the other side of the string, still revolving in the same direction, of course, but now winding the string up. At the top you will catch it in your hand, and fling it again.

The whole secret of throwing the yo-yo, in any direction, and making it return to you, is in the smooth change of direction which you cause and which brings the top back without altering or checking the direction of its spin. Practice will soon give the knack.

CHAPTER FIVE

GAMES EQUIPMENT AND RULES

GAMES EQUIPMENT

Some pieces of equipment are useful for a number of different games. The description of how to prepare such equipment has therefore been left to this special chapter, to avoid repeating the same thing for each separate game. Any of the equipment can be bought from a sports dealer, but you may prefer to make your own things when possible.

Padders. (For games 10, 11, 28, 29, 42, 76.)

A padder is a solid wood racket. It is best made of five-ply or heavy three-ply wood. Cut out the whole shape, including the handle, then thicken the grip by adding a rounded strip of wood to each side of the handle.

The overall length of the padder should be 16½ in., and the greatest width 8½ in. The handle width should be 1 to 1¼ in.

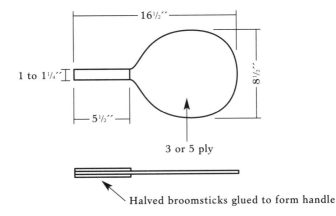

3 or 5 ply

Halved broomsticks glued to form handle

according to taste. The diagram shows shape and detailed measurements. For thickening the handle cut a 5½-in. length of broomstick up the middle and glue or screw to the sides of the plywood.

Court Markings. (For games 9, 10, 11, 22, 24, 26, 34, 36, 38, 40, 41, 42, 44, 45, 47, 48, 49, 50, 57, 58, 65, 66, 73, 75, 76.)

Such markings can, of course, be made with chalk or whitening dissolved in water, but it is far more satisfactory to have tapes which can be taken up or altered at will.

Strong white tape or webbing is needed 1 to 2 in. wide. At the end of each tape should be a staple or pin which can be pushed into the ground. The diagram will show how strong wire or iron should be shaped and pointed so that the tape end can be sewn to it – the pointed ends then push vertically into the ground, so that the tape is taut and flat on the turf.

The most useful length for your tapes is that required for *ring tennis*, for then the same measurements serve for many other net games. Alternatively you may have tapes suitable for *lawn tennis*. The superfluous ends can then be rolled up when unnecessary for smaller court games, and the tape pinned down at the required points by free staples – like that to which the tape is shown sewn in the diagram.

Staple for tapes

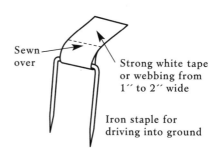

Sewn over

Strong white tape or webbing from 1″ to 2″ wide

Iron staple for driving into ground

Tethered Balls. (For games 15, 16, 19, 29, 48.)

The best plan is to have an ordinary tennis ball and enclose it in a tight net of thin string. The net can be crocheted over the ball, or several lengths of string can be knotted over in rough net form.

Another method is to use a sponge rubber ball. This can be pierced and the string threaded through and knotted at the farther side.

A third plan is to enclose the ball in a thin cloth bag, to which the tethering cord can be attached.

Pole and Socket. (For games 14, 15, 16, 37, 43, 97.)

First get your socket. A 12- to 18-in, piece of heavy galvanized iron piping, with an inside diameter of a little over an inch, is required. This is driven into the ground – care being taken that it is kept upright – until the top end is slightly below the lawn surface. This socket should remain in your lawn, so see that the top is below the reach of mower blades.

Then for your pole or post or peg you simply need more galvanized piping of the appropriate length, correspondingly smaller than the socket, so that it will slide down inside the buried piece and be held firm and upright.

There will naturally be some dirt inside the socket at first, but the small piece of piping will soon ram this down.

Nets. (For games 11, 24, 26, 36, 40, 41, 42, 44, 45, 47, 48, 73, 75, 76.)

Apart from No. 40, *lawn tennis*, all the other games can be served pretty well by a strong net of moderate size. A good plan is to buy a *ring tennis* net – which is sturdy enough for any sort of play. You can have a post 6 ft. high halfway down each side of your lawn, with hooks fixed at various heights. The net can then be attached at whatever height is required for a particular game. It does not really matter if a net does not reach down to the ground – most play is near the top edge.

Beanbags. (For games 3, 52, 53, 78, 96.)

To make a beanbag take two pieces of sateen or similar soft, strong material, each five inches square, and sew them together round the edges, filling between with dried beans, maize or peas. Each bag should contain the same amount of beans – about a couple of handfuls.

Golf Holes. (For games 38, 46, 56, 67.)

A golf hole should be $4\frac{1}{2}$ in. in diameter and at least 4 in. deep.

A small flowerpot serves very well, sunk into the ground so that its top edge is slightly below the ground-level. The hole of the flowerpot is convenient for inserting the flag-stick which marks the position of the hole when players are at a distance. A tin with a hole punched through the bottom will do equally well.

For a quick, makeshift game a tin lid can generally be pressed sufficiently flat to serve as a hole, without digging the turf away.

RULES

The big standard games like *lawn tennis* and *badminton* have their official rules, but there are a large number of garden games played across a net which are not similarly standardized. It is a great convenience to have one set of rules which can apply to all such games – and the following is such a set. Some special, slight adjustments may occasionally be needed to fit particular games, but in the main these will be found to meet all needs.

Net Game Rules. (For games 11, 24, 41, 42, 44, 45, 73, 75, and, with some adaptation, 10, 22, 28, 29, 36, 47, 48, 49.)

1. A *doubles* game has two players on each side of the net; a *singles* has one on each side.

2. In any game where each doubles court is divided down the middle by a line making right and left halves the singles court may or may not have the same line – this will depend on the width available and on personal preference.

3. The size of a doubles court should be 40 ft. by 18 ft. The court markings are shown in the following diagrams.

The 3-ft, strip on either side of the net is 'dead,' just as is the ground right outside the courts.

4. The choice of courts is decided at the commencement of play, by toss, and the side which wins the toss also takes the first service.

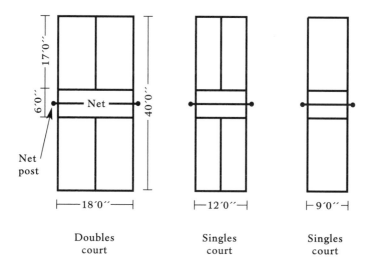

| Doubles court | Singles court | Singles court |

5. The service is delivered alternately from behind the right and left halves of the court, beginning always from the right for the first service.

6. The server's foot must not pass in front of the rear line of the court when a service is being made – a foot is not deemed to be in front if any part of it is touching the line.

7. Service is made over the net to the opponent in the diagonally opposite court. Should the net be touched the service does not count. Two services are allowed, a second being taken if the first is at fault; touching the net does not constitute a fault.

8. A game is won by the player or side which first scores eleven points.

9. When the side that is serving makes a fault – for instance, by failing to get over the net, or getting outside the court – that should not be counted as a point by the opposing side, but instead they should take over the service and begin afresh. Thus only the side that is serving can actually score points, the service simply changing over when they are at fault. Here is an illustration from *ring tennis* play: A wins the toss, and serves from the right-hand court. After some play B returns a throw which A fails to catch. B does not count a point, but instead takes the service, beginning from his right-hand court. The play continues, and then B beats A once more with a fast ring. This time B counts one point, and continues with his services. If the next score is also his, the counting will be 2-*love*. But if after that B fails to catch the ring, letting it fall inside his court, the service goes back to A. Thus only the serving side counts points.

It will be seen that if the score is 10-*all*, and A is serving, then B must score twice in order to reach 11, while A need only score once.

This method eliminates the unfair advantage which one side would have if service were determined only by the toss and were retained throughout a game.

10. In a doubles game the same player takes all the services until the opposite side secures them, but when service comes back to

the first side the other player will take it.

11. After each game the players should change ends.

12. The best of three games wins the *set*.

13. A run may be made before a service is delivered, and after the service players may take up any position they like within their court.

14. Feinting or baulking in any form is forbidden in all play.

15. Stepping over the rear line when serving constitutes a fault, and is counted as one service. Except in services the skimming of the net is of no account.

INDEX

ACKNOWLEDGEMENTS

Executive Editor Trevor Davies

Managing Editor Clare Churly

Executive Art Editor Sally Bond

Cover and endpaper illustrations 'Omedesign

Game illustrations Sudden Impact Media

Page make-up Dorchester Typesetting Group Ltd

Production Controller Carolin Stransky